From AmeriCon to AmeriCan

I0560126

Dr. Dudley Davis

ISBN: 978-1-962624-75-6

Dedication

For my children, who inspired me to write this book so they can experience a better tomorrow.

Acknowledgements

Sincere appreciation to all of the editors and designers who assisted with this project. I value and acknowledge your efforts. In addition, I would like to thank friends and family who supported my work. I am eternally grateful.

About the Author

Dr. Dudley Davis is a writer, speaker, businessman, and social scientist with a master's degree in health psychology, and a Ph.D. in communication research. Throughout his career, Dr. Davis has sought and implemented practical solutions in the areas of diversity, equity, and inclusion, bringing students of all racial and ethnic backgrounds to work together towards making a better America.

Table of Contents

List of Figures

Chapter I

If you can convince the lowest White man he's better than the best colored man, he won't notice you're picking his pocket. Hell, give him somebody to look down on, and he'll empty his pockets for you.

– Lyndon B. Johnson

I was driving with my 15-year-old Black son in our family minivan. It was three in the afternoon and drizzling out. A police car drove by. The white and blue lights flared up. I pulled over and stopped. The White police officer walked over to the driver's side window, "Can I have your license, registration and insurance?" I remained silent and proceeded to provide the documents as requested. The police officer then said, "The reason for my stop is your front light is out and your windshield wiper is going too fast." I looked at the officer in astonishment, but still, I did not say a word. I glanced over at my son in silence and witnessed the sheer bewilderment that overcame his face. It was a good teaching moment for my Black son. The kind of education that many Black parents have with their Black children. The minivan front light was not out, and the sheer ridiculousness of the windshield wiper statement speaks for itself... My Black son's first encounter with a White police officer.

If tomorrow morning you got up out of bed, got struck by lightning on your way to work, and to your surprise, when you awoke, could only see and experience the world from the perspective of a person of color; how would you view the American culture you live in and experience? How would you navigate this system?

The history of race in America is undoubtedly complex and has evolved over centuries, with slavery and Jim Crow laws playing central roles in shaping racial dynamics and social structures. While significant progress has been made, the legacy of slavery and the struggle for racial equality continue to shape America's social and political landscape.

Historical Context: The Experience of Slavery

When I was 11, my mother Linda immigrated from Kingston, Jamaica to the United States in order to make a better life for our family. I was extremely close to my mother, and at the time, like any other 11-year-old boy, she was my world, my all. When she got on the plane without me, I felt my entire world collapsing around me. Those first few nights without her were the longest nights ever. I think I cried for two days straight; the feeling of emptiness was overwhelming and seemingly, could not be filled by anyone else. I can only imagine how it must have felt for kidnapped African children, forced into slavery, to be apart from their parents.

FIGURE 1. First Enslaved Africans Arrive in Jamestown, Virginia. Hulton Archive/Getty Images.[1]

The arrival of the first slave ship to Virginia in 1619 launched the forced migration of Africans to the English colonies in North America.[2] I often imagined what it was like for the first enslaved Africans, stolen away from everything they knew—their home, children, siblings, mother, father, and friends—tethered to other prisoners in chains, sailing across the turbulent seas, and arriving on the American shores. Fear must have overcome them, not knowing what's to come. I can hear the silent screams of children wailing, knowing they will never see their parents again. Olaudah Equiano recounted how he and his sister were abducted when he was 8 years-old:

> One day, when all our people were gone out to their works as usual, and only I and my dear sister were left to mind the house, two men and a woman got over our walls and in a moment seized us both, and, without giving us time to cry out, or make resistance, they stopped our mouths, and ran off with us into the nearest wood. Here they tied our hands, and continued to carry us as far as they could, till night came on, when we reached a small house where the robbers halted for refreshment, and spent the night. We were then unbound, but were unable to take any food; and, being quite overpowered by fatigue and grief, our only relief was some sleep.[3]

This nightmarish account of child abduction was a prevalent occurrence and was only the beginning of an unimaginable ordeal for Olaudah and his sister. The voyage from the coast of Africa to the Americas was horrific, as Equiano further describes this horrifying experience:

> The closeness of the place, and the heat of the climate, added to the number in the ship, which was so crowded that each had scarcely room to turn himself, almost suffocated us…. This wretched situation was again aggravated by the galling of the chains, now become insupportable; and the filth of the necessary tubs, into which the children often fell, and were almost suffocated. The shrieks of the women, and the groans of the

dying, rendered the whole a scene of horror almost inconceivable.[4]

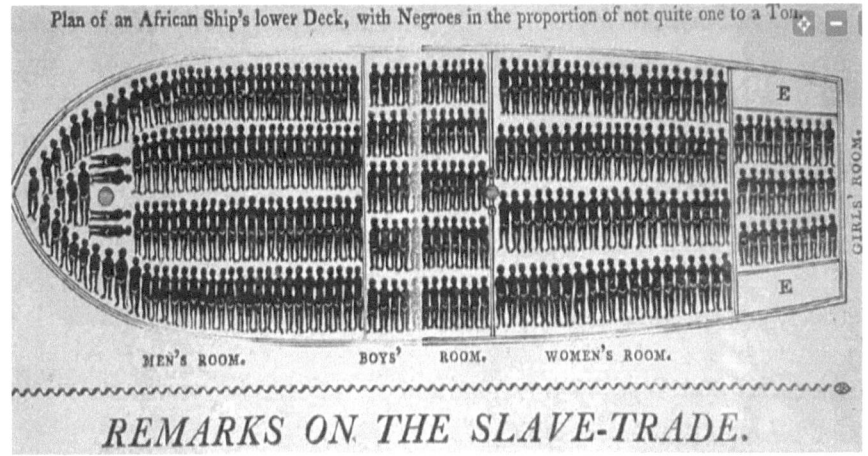

FIGURE 2. Slave ship. Source: Library of Congress.

The transatlantic slave trade, which carried on for the next two centuries, destroyed African families: the forced separation of mothers and children, the rape of women, and the eradication of African cultures by kidnapping Africans from their native lands. One nevertheless has to ask: why is slavery only a footnote in American school textbooks instead of being expounded for the significant role it played in building America's wealth? The uncomfortable topic of race in America will never go away until White historians and politicians stop force-feeding the public their own sanitized version of history in school textbooks, instead of providing a diverse perspective and a true accounting of what really happened.

The System: A Legal Framework of Oppression

Faisal Shah defines a system as a "collection of elements or components that are organized for a common purpose."[5] We live in a well-coordinated system, organized in such a way that only allows one group of people to flourish and feed at the expense of others. The system that I was born in is a system established by White settlers, who organized our politics, our judiciary, our criminal justice, our policing, our housing, and our education system, to strategically divide us by race in the interest of economics and maintenance of White dominance and privilege.[6]

To make these acts palatable, White Americans justified their actions with the Three-Fifths Clause, which is a provision in the United States Constitution that counted each slave as three-fifths of a person for the purposes of determining representation in the U.S. House of Representatives and taxes to be paid to the federal government.[7] The U.S. Supreme Court's 1857 Dred Scott ruling virtually slammed the door shut on Whites seeing Blacks as anything but sub-humans. Nikole Hannah-Jones, a *New York Times* reporter, argues that "The Dred Scott court ruled that Black people, whether enslaved or free, came from a 'slave' race."[8] Everything from the kidnapping of Africans from their native homeland, via their forced servitude, the Three-Fifths Clause and the Dred Scott ruling was fueled by White greed. This 'con' flourished and laid the foundation of unearned privileges for those in power, which persists to this day in American culture and institutions.

I imagined how many African slaves dreamt of being emancipated; yet in 1857, politics trumped the day, legislating them as three-fifths human for the purpose of votes and economic wealth. At that moment, all their hopes and dreams were crushed under the weight of freedom lost. White people's irreverent gaze stole their humanity, reducing their self-worth to chattel, only to be bought and sold. The oppressors sleep comfortably at night, not knowing the unfathomable misery they have caused. Black lives were damaged, irrevocably broken, whose pieces will never be made whole again. The oppressor puts on his Sunday's best, walking along the pews, praying on bended knees, pleading for absolution for sins unrecognized by their God. Their ministers clothed their God in White skin to remind us of this immoral supremacy. They twisted the meaning and intention of words lifted from the Bible to justify the indefensible.

Religious Influence: European Christian Missionaries

I was born in Kingston, Jamaica, in which 92.1% of the population is Black.[8-a] Jamaica gained its independence from British colonizers on August 6, 1962.[9] I was three years-old at the time. From a very early age, I can remember seeing pictures of Jesus, a White blue-eyed Jesus, hanging on the walls of my home. I later realized that this was a strategy, part of White colonists' systematic approach to use religion as another means to control Black and Brown bodies. My mother enrolled my brother and I at St. Theresa elementary, a private White Christian School that was run by the Catholic Church. I remember having White nuns as teachers, with coifs, which framed their faces, and Black veils that ran down their backs and shoulders. I remembered in particular Sister Patrick, a really mean White woman who seemingly had it in for me. Her fat, round, rosy-red cheeks protruded from under her coif, making her look unfriendly, and she had round wired glasses. Sister Patrick singled me out. I could feel her hate. She would discipline me in front of the class, telling me to hold my hands out in front towards her. She would hit my knuckles with the sharp end of the ruler. I stared at her defiantly, taking the pain, never flinching, depriving her of the satisfaction that came with each blow. Sometimes she would take her hands and simultaneously slap both my jaws and ears for my religious defiance. My ears rang from the vibrations of the slap, but I still took the pain. Looking back, I was already rebelling against the system with pride, and I did not even know it. But I knew my view of White people was not monolithic. Out of all the Black kids at St. Theresa, my best friend turned out to be a little blonde-haired White Jamaican boy named Robert. I became really good friends with Robert, and I got the sense he saw me as a rebel who stood firmly against the system.

Rudyard Kipling, a lauded English poet and novelist, in one of his poems, popularized the concept of the "White Man's Burden," which morally justified European Christianity and imperialist expansion in Africa, the West Indies, and other occupied territories. Kipling wrote, "Your new-caught sullen peoples, half-devil and half-child" referring to the European belief that Africans were heathens, resigned to live a life of savagery.[9a] A Scholar Blogs article further explains that "Christianity was one justification that European powers used to colonize and exploit Africa … Essentially, Christianity was a guise by which Western governments justified the exploitation and conquest of African nations."[9b9] This article further points out that Kipling's argument expressed in "The White Man's Burden" was the prevailing mindset for most White Europeans, where they viewed Africans as culturally inferior.

> The idea of the White Man's Burden was to better ("seek another's profit") an ostensibly backward people (anyone who was not White). The lines following this initial declaration reveal the prevailing attitude in regard to how such a civilizing mission would proceed. Kipling bemoans that the African people will come "slowly to the light" and would lament their release from "bondage." In essence, Kipling believed that these non-White racial groups were so backward that they would be unable to comprehend the benefits of Europeanization. It was Kipling's belief that Africans must be pulled toward the "light" in order to see the error of their, in his view, savage nature.[10]

White European colonizers had their footprint all over the Americas and in the West Indies, including Jamaica. In an effort to cultivate and control Blacks in the new territories they were forced to now call home, European missionaries used religion as a tool to bend and mold Blacks to accept and adopt European culture, at the expense of their own. The Black and Brown man have been molded to believe, to see the White man as their savior. This is the damaging psychology, the indoctrination that needs to be reversed. When Black and Brown men resist the White man's tyranny, they are often described through reversed psychology as savages and terrorists by those bent on villainizing them to preserve their status quo. They are master propagandists, who peddle in deceit to justify the insatiable greed they perpetrate against the masses they govern. When the Black and Brown man rebels through the clothes he wears, the language he speaks, or how he chooses to style his hair, it is all questioned against the backdrop of Whiteness. Whiteness then becomes the standard, which was so eloquently stated by Phil in one the sitcom episodes of Modern Family: "If it ain't White, it's ain't right."[11a]

White Supremacy and The Con

Kaleigh Howland claims that "White supremacy is not just some extremist movement, … White supremacy is among the foundational principles of our country."[11] For the purpose of this book, White supremacy is defined as a culture where almost everything in society is seen and valued through the system of Whiteness. I argue that the very foundation of America's power culture was built on a con of White supremacy. According to the Cambridge Dictionary, the word "con" means to trick, deceive, or make someone believe something that is known to be false.[12] This con was designed to convince Americans born with White skin that they are racially superior to those with Black and Brown skin; a con indoctrinated strategically and propagated for centuries through the media, schools, families, religion, politicians, literature, and other institutions in American society. The con has been so thorough, that if one took the least accomplished White person, and compared them to the most accomplished Black person, society conditions us to favor the former by default.

In his study on anti-Black biases in America, Michael Rizzo found that explicit anti-Black biases emerge early and continue to develop throughout childhood.[13] Rizzo states that "By 4 to 5 years of age, children—and White children in particular—hold more negative attitudes toward Black than White peers, attribute more negative intentions to Black than White peers, and are less likely to form friendships with Black than White peers."[14] Furthermore, Rizzo argued, "Consistent with past research, children were least likely to choose to play with the Black child and did so significantly less often than expected by chance. Children also chose to play with the Latino/a child less often than expected by chance."[15] Growing up with these conscious and unconscious biases, these are the children who become our police officers, judges, politicians, bankers, and employers—gatekeepers of a system that rails against Black and Brown bodies.

This malicious con of White supremacy is viral in nature, metastasizing across the land through our collective unconscious. It has infected our values, our books, our beliefs and our children, ultimately manifesting in our behavior and actions. From the very first day, a White child draws their first breath, the system elevates them over their Black and Brown brothers and sisters. The system is intentionally crafted to lift one class of Americans over another in housing, schooling, banking, policing and the criminal justice system, which has yielded devastating generational consequences for Black and Brown Americans.[16] This legalized oppressive system gave unfair racial and economic preference to Whites, setting them up financially for generations. For example, one only need to look at the federal government's collusion with White businesses, where they conspired and codified laws to prevent Black and Brown citizens from acquiring property in the course of the twentieth century. Larry Adelman provided a detailed accounting of this collusion:

Less known are more recent government racial preferences, first enacted during the New Deal, that directed wealth to white families and continue to shape life opportunities and chances today.

The landmark Social Security Act of 1935 provided a safety net for millions of workers, guaranteeing them an income after retirement. But the act specifically excluded two occupations: agricultural workers and domestic servants, who were predominately African American, Mexican, and Asian. As low-income workers, they also had the least opportunity to save for their retirement. They couldn't pass wealth on to their children. Just the opposite. Their children had to support them.

Like Social Security, the 1935 Wagner Act helped establish an important new right for white people. By granting unions the power of collective bargaining, it helped millions of white workers gain entry into the middle class over the next 30 years. But the Wagner Act permitted unions to exclude non-whites and deny them access to better paid jobs and union protections and benefits such as health care, job security, and pensions. Many craft unions remained nearly all-white well into the 1970s. In 1972, for example, every single one of the 3,000 members of Los Angeles Steam Fitters Local #250 was still white.

But it was another racialized New Deal program, the Federal Housing Administration, that helped generate much of the wealth that so many white families enjoy today. These revolutionary programs made it possible for millions of average white Americans—but not others—to own a home for the first time. The government set up a national neighborhood appraisal system, explicitly tying mortgage eligibility to race. Integrated communities were ipso facto deemed a financial risk and made ineligible for home loans, a policy known today as "redlining." Between 1934 and 1962, the federal government backed $120 billion of home loans. More than 98% went to whites. Of the 350,000 new homes built with federal support in northern

California between 1946 and 1960, fewer than 100 went to African Americans.

These government programs made possible the new segregated white suburbs that sprang up around the country after World War II. Government subsidies for municipal services helped develop and enhance these suburbs further, in turn fueling commercial investments. Freeways tied the new suburbs to central business districts, but they often cut through and destroyed the vitality of non-white neighborhoods in the central city.

Today, Black and Latino mortgage applicants are still 60% more likely than whites to be turned down for a loan, even after controlling for employment, financial, and neighborhood factors. According to the Census, whites are more likely to be segregated than any other group. As recently as 1993, 86% of suburban whites still lived in neighborhoods with a black population of less than 1%.

One result of the generations of preferential treatment for whites is that a typical white family today has on average eight times the assets, or net worth, of a typical African American family, according to New York University economist Edward Wolff. Even when families of the same income are compared, white families have more than twice the wealth of Black families. Much of that wealth difference can be attributed to the value of one's home, and how much one inherited from parents.[17]

These malignant practices have led to generational poverty for many Black and Brown families, in addition to being blamed for not rolling up their sleeves and pulling themselves out of poverty like other hard-working Americans. Left in a constant state of oppression, the oppressed are locked into a psychological spiral of needing to prove their worth, a feat never attainable in the eyes of the oppressor. A government that financially schemes in favor of one citizen over another is akin to a parent who favors one child over another. This unwittingly creates a climate of resentment among siblings, and the child who finds herself disfavored is in constant need to prove her value, invisible to the parent's gaze, which is rather transfixed on the favored child who commands it. These illegitimate practices inevitably created a social class structure, putting White people as the privileged class, and Black and Brown people as lower-class. To accomplish this feat, the system had to create a legal basis to legitimize its actions and codified them into laws.[18] Once these laws were enacted by local, state, and federal legislators, and codified into policies and laws, this illegitimate system used its police force, federal system, private banking, housing segregation, separate and unequal education practice, to create this virulent virus that still contaminates and eats away at the American civic body. Whites and people of color have been useful robots in a system that requires them to remain silent, never challenging the privileges bestowed on those fortunate to have or not have them, reduced to fighting for crumbs while the fat cats who run this con (system) build their empires, nobly admired by society for their savviness and business acumen. This is the nature of the American "con" that holds Black and Brown people in a constant state of oppression, and the mindless collusion of unsuspecting Whites who go along with this ruse. Thus, the overriding question to ponder is, do American institutions play critical roles in upholding White supremacy in America's power culture?

Chapter II

Few American institutions have so excluded minority group members from influence and control as have the news media. This failure is reflected by general insensitivity and indifference and is verified by ownership, management, and employment statistics.

−U. S. Department of Justice Community Relations Service Report, 1969 (Bell, 2022).

Media: Propagating the Con

Back in the early 1970s, I remember watching the television series *Daniel Boone*, which cast Indians as villains. I remembered part of the series theme song lyrics, "… Daniel Boone was a man. Yes, a big man. And he fought for America to make all Americans free."[19] In reflection, I remember buying into the con. I found myself rooting for the White hero, Daniel Boone, bravely protecting the White heroine, whose home was being attacked by the villainous marauding Indians. Years later when my view of the world matured, this irony could not be starker. In my developing worldview, I became keenly aware that whoever told the story, made all the difference in the world. I was even more aware that the story would be entirely different, and would have left me with a different perspective, were the writers and producers of the *Daniel Boone* series Native Americans. For the first time, I began to understand the unmatched power that the media wields to shape minds, reinforce values, and influence the masses.[20]

I also became more cognizant of the few cameo appearances of Black and Brown faces on television, and that they were often depicted not how they see themselves, but how White producers chose to portray them. I became aware that White people, who have never been in the company of Black and Brown people, and in the absence of such real experience, will defer to the powerful images and message the media portrayed. As my worldview crystalized, I realized this endless supply of racialized oxygen is what keeps the ideology of White supremacy alive. I realized White people's perception of me was not my reality, was not how I saw myself. It was then that I made up my mind to challenge the mis-characterization and perception of Black and Brown people.

Marshall McLuhan, a Canadian philosopher and communications theorist, argued that the medium through which information is conveyed shapes the way people perceive and understand it. He believed that the media has the power to shape our social and cultural norms and values, including our attitudes towards race.

McLuhan did not specifically address the issue of racism in his work, but he did discuss the role of the media in creating and reinforcing stereotypes. McLuhan argued the medium itself shapes how we understand and interpret the message being conveyed,[21] which I believe can lead to the reinforcement of harmful stereotypes and biases. In other words, even if the medium, which in this case is the news and entertainment media, provides a false narrative, people will believe it must be true. The media helps shape how we interpret messages, which often are harmful stereotypes that negatively impact Black and Brown people.

The use of the media to push White supremacy is not a new phenomenon; rather, this practice has been prevalent throughout American history. In early America, the media was a huge propaganda tool to justify White colonialism and the enslavement of people of color. More recently, the media has been used to fuel the rise of White supremacist groups, and push racist policies forward.[22] As Kaleigh Howland argues, "news media organizations play both an active and complicit role in White supremacy by minimizing people of color's voices in news coverage and taking a 'both sides' approach to racists."[23] Some examples include "coddling and normalizing bigots" while giving off the appearance of real concern for Black and Brown people. However, the true face of the media often reveals itself by their frequent portrayal of people of color as criminals, or as a burden to society, and the idea that immigration is a threat to national security.

Throughout American history, the media had been complicit with other institutions (i.e., police, judicial systems, political organizations) in promoting White supremacy. It is estimated that during the era of slavery, U.S. newspapers published more than 200,000 paid runaway-slave ads.[24] Alicia Bell points to the complicit role the media played during the era of slavery in America:

> Media organizations were complicit in the slave trade and profited off of chattel slavery; a powerful newspaper publisher helped lead the deadly overthrow of a local government in Wilmington, North Carolina, where Black people held power throughout the city; racist journalism has led to countless lynchings; Southern broadcast stations aired vociferous opposition to integration; and, in the 21st century, powerful social-media and companies are allowing white supremacists to use their platforms to organize, recruit and spread violent hate.[25]

Collette Watson of the Free Press found evidence that showed newspapers were used to catch enslaved Black people, and in the 1950s and 1960s, media giant AT&T colluded with the police and the FBI to surveil Black activists.[26] Watson claims there exists a propagating narrative in the United States, namely that "Black folks are a danger to this country," which has been osmotically permeating American culture for centuries through White media owners.[27] This pattern, she argues, persists to this day through online social media platforms that shape the conflict, generate revenues, and synthesize online traffic.[28] Watson further articulates how the media is weaponized to craft a narrative that is harmful to people of color:

> Our media system is the same as any other system in this country: It wasn't created to help Black folks; it was created to harm Black folks. From the first continuous newspaper to the present day, the media system has worked to uphold a White-racial hierarchy ... Its goal has always been to create a myth of Black inferiority. Narratives are a political tool that have been weaponized to harm Black and Indigenous folks and other people of color ... We have a narrative that Black folks are a danger to this country, and that narrative has carried on for centuries because we mainly have White media owners. And now we see it in the algorithms and how online platforms use these narratives to shape conflict in order to synthesize traffic.[29]

In its current state, the American media is not a friend to my Black son and daughters. I understand no industry is monolithic in its thinking, and therefore I recognize that there are some fair-minded journalists wanting to do the right thing and do unbiased reporting. I have also not lost sight of the fact that these journalists are trapped in a biased system, which they have no control over. Nonetheless, it is my belief, that in its current state and form the media is there to uphold White-racial hierarchy while reinforcing the myth of Black and Brown inferiority. This is illustrated when the media perpetuates White supremacy by underrepresenting or ignoring the viewpoints or experiences of Black and Brown people, while acknowledging and displaying empathetic reporting for White people.

Crafting Perception

In a recent report that looked at media coverage of criminal defendants in the U.S., racial bias was found in over 20 different categories.[30] Some of these categories included "the use of imagery, language choices, the framing of the accused and the victim, and reporter background."[31] Bryan Stevenson, director of the Equal Justice Initiative, claims that "News media have often reinforced a presumption of guilt and dangerousness assigned to Black people when reporting on crime while devaluing the lives of Black people and the harm they suffer when victimized. American media can and should do better in eliminating racially biased coverage."[32] Some of the findings from the report include:

- Mugshots were used in coverage of 45% of cases involving Black people accused of crimes compared to only 8% of cases involving White defendants.
- White victims were nearly four times more likely to be presented in photos with friends and family than Black people victimized by crime.
- Media coverage was 50% more likely to refer to White defendants by name as compared to Black defendants.[33]

Jenée Desmond-Harris alleged that television stations in New York City gave disproportionate coverage to crimes involving Black suspects. In her article, Desmond-Harris alleges that a number of New York television stations "used their late-night broadcasts to report on murder, theft, and assault cases with Black suspects at much higher rates than Black suspects were actually arrested for those crimes."[34]

FIGURE 3. Two sets of Crime photos. Photo: Dennis Clifton (Desmond-Harris, 2015).

"What people see and hear in the media has a tremendous effect on their lives," Robinson said. "It has a tremendous effect on decisions they make, from decisions that are made in the schoolhouse to the courthouse… when Iowa sister news sites TheGazette.com and KCRG.com published stories about two groups of men—one Black and one White—arrested for burglary last week, it didn't take long for readers to start asking why the White suspects were pictured in suits and ties (their wrestling team photos), while photos accompanying the story about the Black suspects were mug shots.[35]

In figure 3, if you do not have a problem with the images displayed, then I submit, *you* are the problem. How can these images be justified for the same crimes? This is the fear that keeps Black and Brown parents awake at night. We have not lost sight of how those in the media view our Black and Brown sons and daughters with a tainted lens, while intentionally presenting a sanitized image of Whiteness. To be clear, the media, in its current state, indoctrinates unsuspecting Whites to fear Black people. This indoctrination takes the form of shaping perceptions and attitudes through the stories it chooses to tell and how it chooses to tell them. Research has shown that the media can perpetuate stereotypes and bias, including the portrayal of Black and Brown people as dangerous criminals.[36] Spike Lee, one of the few African American Hollywood movie producers, craftily demonstrated through his on-screen characters how racial indoctrination is subtly introduced, accepted as factual, and spreads throughout our society via print and visual media.

In Spike Lee's 1992 movie, *Malcolm X*, one of the main characters described how the con, the indoctrination, is subtly disseminated through one of the most respected print media, the *Webster College Dictionary*. In one scene, the character attempts to explain to Malcolm X how he has been duped by the system to hate himself. He hands Malcolm X the dictionary to study how the word "black" is defined, and compare it to how "white" is defined:

> Black—destitute of light. Devoid of color. Enveloped in darkness. Hence, utterly dismal, or gloomy. As the future looks black. Soiled with dirt. Foul, sullen, hostile. Forbidding, as a black day. Foully or outrageously wicked, as black cruelty. Indicating disgrace, dishonor, or culpability. And there are others, blackmail, blackball, blackguard...

> Let's look up white.

> White. Of the color of pure snow. Reflecting all the rays of the spectrum. The opposite of black. Free from spots or blemishes. Innocent. Pure. Without evil intent. Harmless. Honest. Square-dealing and honorable.[37]

Even when disaster hits, and Americans are at their most vulnerable, the American media is never asleep at the wheel and stands ready to divide us through its constant indoctrination. This was the case in New Orleans, Louisiana during Hurricane Katrina in 2005.

FIGURE 4. "White People 'Find,' Black People 'Loot.'"
AFP/Getty Images; Photo image/Associated Press – Chris Graythen.

Figure 4 illustrates blatantly biased reporting during the 2005 Hurricane Katrina disaster in New Orleans, Louisiana. In the image on the left, media outlets reported on two White residents wading through chest-deep water to *find* bread and soda. In the image on the right, under the same circumstances, media outlets reported on a young man (clearly visible as Black) wading through chest-deep water after *looting* a grocery store.[38] This is how the con works in the media. The problem presented here with biased media in America could not be any plainer. This irresponsible, evil reporting has consequences, and frames how Black and Brown people are perceived, criminalized, and incarcerated at alarming rates in the United States. Knowing what you know about race in America, which White person would willingly trade places with a Black person? We all know all too well what the answer to this rhetorical question would be. The people who willingly and complicitly apply the weight of injustice on the backs of minorities, seemingly cannot elevate their conscience to a level of compassion to relieve a burden they themselves would not bear. America will only rise to meet its promise when compassion wears no color, when justice is indeed blind, and racial superiority becomes the enemy of the masses.

Chapter III

We must not only learn to tolerate our differences. We must welcome them as the richness and diversity which can lead to true intelligence.

–Albert Einstein

Education: Reinforcing the Con (Whites' Only Version of History)

My three American-born children attended elementary school in the Northeast, but it could have been anywhere in the United States. Their history textbook is called "American History," but gleaning through the pages, the stories told are overwhelming of one race of people. My children saw no likeness or images of Black, Brown, or other people of color. My children learned or read nothing of their peoples' accomplishments or the inhumane experiences they had to endure; likewise absent from these pages was the savagery that other races had to endure. I worried about the impact this experience would have on my children. No role models, their own history omitted and buried. There is an obsession with Whiteness— whiteness drunk with indoctrination and an unquenchable thirst to be supreme. No one in authority questions this lunacy with the provocative questions: Why are there no other races included in

America's history books? Why is there no true accounting of what actually happened?

My son who attended a predominantly White elementary school recounted to me, whenever the topic of slavery or the Civil Rights era was glanced over in his classroom, all eyes zoomed in on him, like the lens of a camera, focused to detect his slightest emotional reaction. It was not clear to him whether the White faces in the room were displaying dominance, empathy, arrogance, apathy, or revulsion of past deeds. The unwanted glares make him the center of attention. The air in the room was charged with uncomfortable silence. His body, ever so slightly, sank in his seat from the unwanted gaze, carrying the weight of his skin. It is heavy.

Cheated

'Cheated' is the only word that comes to mind when I think about the accomplishments of Katherine Johnson, one of the great African American mathematicians of our time who helped NASA launch space exploration. Her story only came to light through the 2016 movie, Hidden Figures. The question is, why are we learning about her story now? Why was her story, and those of the many other African Americans who helped NASA, absent from our history books?

The American educational system cheats students of color of their role models. You cannot aspire to what you do not see. What the American education system has been allowed to perpetrate on students of color is a travesty. The American education system, from kindergarten on up, would have you believe no other people have contributed to the success of this nation other than White Americans. America has been too comfortable force-feeding White only history on its non-White population, while propping up barriers that prevent the teachings of multi-racial history in American schools.[39] When you deliberately suppress the accomplishments of role models, America loses, for it loses the next generation of innovators who rely on role models to propel them to their zenith. White students have the luxury and privilege to learn about their forebears and role models in schools through history books, while Native Americans, Blacks, and Brown peoples' contributions' have been deliberately left out, leaving no other role models other than White ones, which the privileged majority wants you to commemorate. Look around, the conservative far right have made it painstakingly clear: they have no intentions of budging when it comes to culturally diversifying what is being taught in American schools.[40]

One has to ask the question, why is slavery cited as a footnote in American school textbooks instead of expounding on the significant role it played in building America's wealth?[41] America hides from its past, fearing the truth of past deeds will be too much for American students to bear. Ron DeSantis, the Governor of Florida, recently passed the "Stop W.O.K.E. Act" which states, "curriculum may not be used to indoctrinate or persuade students" and seeks to ensure that no child feels "guilt or anguish" or "psychological distress" during lessons on topics like slavery in America".[41a] America will never become whole until it chooses to reckon with its past. Historian Donald Yacovone, an associate at the Hutchins Center for African & African American Research, made a cogent appeal for diversifying American textbooks:

> If America is to be a nation that fulfills its democratic promise, the history of slavery and white supremacy have to be taught in schools across the country. We need to acknowledge that white supremacy remains an integral part of American society and we need to understand how we got to where we are. The consequences of not doing so are lethal. White supremacy is a toxin. The older history textbooks were like syringes that injected the toxin of white supremacy into the mind of many

generations of Americans. What has to be done is teach the truth about slavery as a central institution in America's origins, as the cause of the Civil War, and about its legacy that still lives on. The consequences of not doing so, we're seeing every day.[42]

Unfriendly Spaces

According to Julia McEvoy, an *NPR* reporter, "Racist bullying on high school campuses is on the rise. The increase comes as more rural residents identify as multiracial and their children are attending majority white schools that can be hostile."[43] Racism among students in American schools has been a long-standing issue that can contribute to an unfriendly and hostile environment for minority students. McEvoy went on to share an incident that occurred with several of the students in her article:

> MCEVOY: Last month things really blew up when a racist prom proposal from a white student hit Instagram and made the rounds in the community. Jerry Loya saw the post.
>
> LOYA: It said, if I were Black, I'd be picking cotton, but I'm not, so I'm picking you. It's just blatant racism that—she wasn't even trying to hide it.[44]

These incidents have occurred in my own backyard. My 16-year-old son, John, attended a predominantly White high school. During recess on the playground, my son was with a group of his White friends. They were all shooting the breeze and talking about sports.

John decided to speak up and gave his two-cents worth on the topic, when one of the boys turned to him and said cavalierly, "you're Black, your opinion doesn't matter." Laughter erupted among the other White boys. John fell silent, embarrassed by the moment that unexpectedly accosted him. There were no rocks close by where he could crawl under. That moment clothed him in derision. John felt alone, a speck of black floating in a sea of milk. He was an outsider. Silence was his only friend. Many more incidents followed.

In another incident, John was at lunch with one of his White classmates. John had thought highly of his friend, Rob, who was always cool and nice to him, but during one of their conversations Rob made an unexpected remark to John, apparently jokingly, "well, you are 3/5th of a person." John froze, perplexed by the words spoken by a supposed friend. No words escaped John's mouth. Rob knew his words had hit a raw nerve, sending shockwaves through John's body. Rob instantly regretted what he had said, even if it was in jest. He realized the impact of his words on John, for slavery had already dealt a mortal wound to the souls of Black people. Rob begged John not to tell school administrators what he had said.

The final incident that I will share occurred during John's lunch break, when one of his five White classmates, Mick, called him over to their table. Mick then proceeded to pull out an audio app on his phone of a "whip cracking sound," while striking down towards John, as if to portray whipping him like a slave master. Everyone around the table erupted with laughter. When recounting this story John said, "that sh-- never leaves you once you experience it." Then he looked over at me and said, "It's time. I want out."

Racialized Discipline

Black students are 3.8 times more likely than White students to receive a school suspension, according to the U.S. Department of Education's Office of Civil Rights. This is not because students of color cause more problems; rather, it is because Black students receive disproportionate punishment even after socioeconomic status, achievement, self-reported behavior, and teacher-reported behavior are taken into account.[45] As a Black parent, I experienced and read about the discrepancy between how Black children are disciplined in American schools, compared to White children.[46] Disciplined for how they look, what they wear, and how they speak.

I remembered an incident that my daughter, Elizabeth, had with a White student in high school, who I will call Marie. Marie had used the racial epithet, 'N----r,' profusely on her social media account. There was documented proof and screen shots of the incident that Elizabeth had shared with me. The next day, Elizabeth, at some point confronted Marie and questioned her use of the "N" word. Things dramatically changed after this encounter.

At lunch break, Marie was sitting across the room at a table with her friends, and Elizabeth was sitting with her friends, three tables away. No words were ever spoken at lunch between Elizabeth and Marie. Yet, at some point that afternoon, Elizabeth was summoned to the vice-principal's office for allegedly intimidating Marie by "staring at her in a threatening manner." I became livid and contacted the principal's office through my lawyer, demanding answers to why Elizabeth was called into the office and not Marie for what she had done. The school administration quietly dropped the issue, as did I. This incident reinforced how White school administrators will quickly run to the aid of White students, at the expense of Black and Brown students, without fully vetting the facts to what occurred.

I later learned of a new national study that suggests an increase in discipline or achievement gaps between Black and White students may have a cause-and-effect relationship.[47] In other words, "As the racial discipline gap goes up, so too does the racial achievement gap...Likewise, as the racial discipline gap goes down, so too does the racial achievement gap."[48] I worried how this new information impacted my children and the many other students of color throughout this nation.

Intelligence Questioned

Education was highly prized in my family. My mother set the tone, saved up what little money she had in Jamaica to send my brother and I to the best schools. I attended public schools in New York City, graduated and moved away to college in New England. In my first year in college, I attended a community college in the Northeast and played on the basketball team where I was the "star;" in my first semester on the team, I became the leading scorer. At the same time, my schoolwork was taking a hit and was not my priority, and in short order my GPA dropped below the required number, and I got kicked off the team and placed on academic probation. I was deeply embarrassed, because it was in the newspapers, and I knew that was not who I was nor wanted to represent as a person of color.

In America, when a Black man fails to meet the educational standards set by the White ruling class, he is automatically assumed to be dumb, intellectually inferior, and uneducated. I was keenly aware of this stigma when I was put on academic probation. I knew this had nothing to do with my intellect, but rather my lack of focus in the classroom. I changed the narrative in quick order, studied hard and got off academic probation, and was reinstated back on the team by the next semester. I never forgot that lesson and I vowed never to allow myself to fall below the academic standards I set for myself. In later years, I went on to fulfill my academic ambition and received a master's degree and a PhD from two distinguished American institutions.

White intelligence is the cornerstone of the con. For too long this con has fueled the notion that if people of color were allowed equal access in schools and businesses, this would compromise quality. The system makes sure that the one message that gets through is the White race's intelligence. The idea that certain races are inherently more intelligent than others is a racist belief that has been discredited by scientific research.[49] Historically, however, this belief was used to justify discriminatory practices and policies, including in the American education system. For example, schools in the United States were often segregated and resources were not distributed equally; a practice that still continues to this day, which has enormous educational implications for students of color.[50] Additionally, racist ideologies were taught in some schools, which perpetuate harmful stereotypes and reinforce the belief in the supposed intellectual inferiority of Black people.[51]

Standardized testing became foundational for the American school system over a century ago.[52] The real question has always been, who designed these tests and what was their motivation? John Rosales and Tim Walker from the Nation Education Association argued that "To tell the truth about standardized tests ... is to tell the story of the eugenicists who created and popularized these tests in the United States more than a century ago."[53] Many of these scientists were White Anglo-Saxon Protestants who positioned the White race at the very top, which reeked of bias and self-serving privileges.[54] White teachers who have been organically indoctrinated in the culture of Whiteness will inevitable require students of color to conform to their standards and values. A good example of this is, as an article in Columbia University's Teachers College stated, "White teachers, for example, frequently admonish their African American students to 'leave your cultural baggage at home and don't bring it into the classroom.' They have little awareness that they bring their Whiteness into the classroom and operate from a predominantly White ethnocentric perspective."[55]

In his 1923 book, *A Study of American Intelligence,* psychologist and eugenicist Carl Brigham argued that "the Nordic race group" is superior, and intermingling new immigrants in the American gene pool is not a good thing.[56] For decades, these biased instruments have been used to limit Black and Brown students access to America's prestigious schools, thus providing an unfair advantage to the White privileged class. Rosales and Walker suggest that instead of focusing on the aptitude of Black and Brown children, we should really be looking at the racial biases and flaws in the instruments we are using in standardized testing. "We still think there's something wrong with the kids rather than recognizing their something wrong with the tests," Ibram X. Kendi of the Antiracist Research and Policy Center at Boston University and author of *How to be an Antiracist* said in October 2020. "Standardized tests have become the most effective racist weapon ever devised to objectively degrade Black and Brown minds and legally exclude their bodies from prestigious schools."[57]

Shaping Language To Fit In With the Dominant Culture

In America's power culture, the message has always been clear to Black and Brown people: there is only one path to success in America, and it is through the path of the White power culture. You either learn how to speak, write, and acclimate to the accepted norms of the White culture or you will not flourish, or worse, not survive in this society. What White people are asking of people of color is to live a lie that weakens their heritage, to make them feel uncomfortable in their own skin. As Calvin John Smiley and David Fakunle point out, "Over the last several years, the term 'thug' has become a way to describe Black males who reject or do not rise to the standard of White America."[58] The closer our lives mirror the White man's life, the less threatened he feels. Yet, he does not want you to mirror his life to the point where you surpass his accomplishments or material wealth, for he needs, always, to be seated at the head of the table. Ask yourselves, whose culture is being reflected in the mirror when you rise in the morning, and understand there are two roads, one of assimilation and the other of your ancestral heritage. Whichever road you choose to take, there is a social and psychological cost. The latter may be unsustainable.

Black and Brown people have had to learn how to survive and function in a White dominated culture, which provides an innate advantage to White children. I have often wondered why those critical of Black and Brown children have not pondered why these children struggle to function in a system that is disadvantageous to them. Lev Vygotsky, a pioneer of the sociocultural theory of cognitive development, argued that learning is embedded within social events, and social interaction plays a fundamental role in the improvement of learning.[59] For example, the lexicon used in Black households is drastically different than the one used in White households, which impacts learning and is strategically advantageous to White children who are raised and expected to perform by the metrics set by America's White culture.[60] John Steinbeck's *Of Mice and Men* or Ernest Hemingway's *For Whom the Bell Toll* are not the kind of literature discussed in Black and Brown families, yet it may be the kind of literature question they run into on a standardized test.

I argue that if one accepts Lev Vygotsky's theory that learning is a function of our social environment, then one may extrapolate that if a White child is socialized and reared in a White household, where the family discussion revolves around the performance of the stock market and finance, that child most likely will do well in their professional career in this field. In essence, Vygotsky argues, that the manner in which we are socialized early in life by our respective cultures directly impacts our knowledge. It follows that Black and Brown children's performance on standardized test with metrics set by White culture will ultimately produce outcomes unfavorable to Black and Brown students. As I pointed out in one of my papers:

> The burden is never placed on teachers to culturally understand that this gap exists (Lim & Renshaw, 2001), not because the intellectual capacity is not there, but rather a mountainous burden is placed on African American students to catch up, make up the distance, and learn an unfamiliar culture's language in a short period of time in order to competitively compete, pass, and function. The argument being made here is that it has taken White students all their lives to live, learn and fully grasp what is expected educationally from the dominant White culture; African American students are expected to learn this in a few short years in the educational system. Unfortunately, there are going to be

many African American casualties (attrition) because White teachers are not aware of this cultural divide and will often misdiagnose the problem (Lim and Renshaw (2001).[61]

Mocking the Language of Black Culture

Have you ever heard a White person complimenting an African American by saying "You speak so well"?[62] Just dissect the implications of that meaning. This is, at a minimum, a backhanded indictment of the linguist value Whites see in the African American cultural communication process. There is a tacit disdain for the African American language, where it is seen by the White power culture as inferior, uneducated, and uncultured. The African American who can successfully code switch, namely, to shift from speaking Black lingo to speaking White standard English well in the company of Whites, are recognized and rewarded by the White power culture with compliments like, "you are different, you don't speak like them." This biased mindset runs rampant in educational settings, where it is not only expected to speak the language, but also demanded, and you cannot pass through that gauntlet to graduate until you do. Nicole Holliday and Lauren Squires argue that higher education institutions are historically predominantly- and socioeconomically-privileged domains for White people, and have shown White supremacist patterns throughout American educational systems.[63] Holliday and Squires further suggest that by the time Black students reach college, they have been well-conditioned, trained and oriented on Standardized English and are comfortable speaking and writing in it, regardless of their attitudinal orientations toward linguistic varieties.

American classrooms overwhelmingly insist on "Standardized English" as the sole mode of instruction and learning, creating a system of privilege that benefits those who enter school speaking it. For Black students without Standardized English as part of their repertoire, experiencing negative consequences on learning outcomes and self-esteem are well-documented. Schools are among the institutions that reproduce what Baker-Bell (2020) terms 'anti-black linguistic racism.'[64] Most recently, LeBron James, the National Basketball Association superstar was told to "shut up and dribble" by Fox News host Laura Ingraham, when he spoke out on political issues regarding Black Lives Matter: "Ingraham responded to his comments Thursday, calling them 'barely intelligible' and 'ungrammatical' on her Fox News program *The Ingraham Angle.* 'It's always unwise to seek political advice from someone who gets paid $100 million a year to bounce a ball,' she said. 'Keep the political comments to yourselves…. Shut up and dribble.'"[65]

Laura Ingraham's subtle racial message about LeBron James to her Fox News viewing audience was obvious to Black and Brown people. Her referencing his words as "barely intelligible" and "ungrammatical" was code for, "You are unintelligent. Learn to speak our language," and clearly coming from a position of superiority. LeBron James' response back to Laura Ingraham was swift and to the point: "We will definitely not shut up and dribble…. I mean too much to society, too much to the youth, too much to so many kids who feel like they don't have a way out."[66]

The dialogue from the Jive guys in [AIRPLANE] was meticulously researched by the actors with books about Black language.

Second Jive Dude Al White said of the process: "I went and got a couple of books—one was on black English by J.L. Dillard, and another was on black language...and tried to come up with what I felt was jive... using actual words and actual meaning... It's not a bunch of gibberish or whatever. It did actually mean something."

CRACKED.com

FIGURE 5. Jive Talk from the Movie *Airplane*. Photo/Source: YouTube.67

To some Whites, the use of Black language is only acceptable if it has entertainment value and can be made fun of. Historically, Black language has been a component of widespread racial stereotypes and derision on television, like "jive talk" (see figure 5).[68] The main message being that people who speak that way are uneducated, unrefined, thugs, and associated with being from a lower socioeconomic class.[69]

The buzz over the summer blockbuster "Transformers: Revenge of the Fallen" only grew Wednesday as some said two jive-talking Chevy characters were racial caricatures. Skids and Mudflap, twin robots disguised as compact hatchbacks, constantly brawl and bicker in rap-inspired street slang. They're forced to acknowledge that they can't read. One has a gold tooth. As good guys, they fight alongside the Autobots and are intended to provide comic relief. But their traits raise the specter of stereotypes most notably seen when Jar Jar Binks, the clumsy, broken-English speaking alien from "Star Wars: Episode I — The Phantom Menace," was criticized as a caricature. One fan called the Transformers twins "Jar Jar Bots" in a blog post online. Todd Herrold, who watched the movie in New York City, called the characters "outrageous." "It's one thing when robot cars are racial stereotypes," he said, "but the movie also had a bucktoothed Black guy who is briefly in one scene who's also a stereotype." "They're like the fools," said 18-year-old Nicholas Govede, also of New York City. "The comic relief in a degrading way."[70]

Jada Vasser of *The State News* defined code-switching as, "the practice of alternating between two or more languages or varieties of language in conversation."[71] Vasser states that code-switching is "used by the Black community to eliminate bias and stereotypes towards them, especially in non-Black dominant spaces."[72] In other words, we use code-switching to fit in, get in, or be accepted in White spaces. Oftentimes we code-switch with more than our words. Sometimes we code-switch with what we wear or who we write to.[73] At a national conference I attended on race and ethnicity, one of the attendees stated that he code-switched to make himself "invisible." Another presenter implied that code-switching is a death sentence for some. He said he had code-switched away from his community and original identity, where he was not able to find his way back, the implication being that there should be a clear line drawn between code-switching and assimilation. Assimilation comes at a dire cost, where the White power culture forces you to lose your identity and adopt theirs. Shouldn't there be room for both cultures? Every culture has value and brings something to the table. Black and Brown people are required to code-switch in order to flourish and realize the American dream; but again, I ask, why are Whites not required to code-switch? I think we all know the answer to that question.

Black and Brown rap and hip-hop artists are, perhaps, the single monolith group that resist code-switching en masse. This is probably due to the street credit they garner with young followers who rebelliously buy into their ant-establishment message. From their rap lyrics, gaudy jewelry, and baggy pants that often sit below their butts, Black and Brown rap and hip-hop artists, seemingly defy the insurmountable pressure to code-switch in order to find financial

success in contemporary White American culture.[74]

Chapter IV

Every society gets the kind of criminal it deserves. What is equally true is that every community gets the kind of law enforcement it insists on.

–Robert Kennedy

American Justice: The Criminalization of Black and Brown People

My first run in with the law was in Times Square in New York City in the mid-1970s. I was 16 years-old at the time. I was headed back home and decided to take the Subway N train back home. I think at the time, the fee for riding the train was 35 cents. I had the 35 cents on me, but for some unknown reason, I decided to do something I had never done before—jump the turnstile and not pay. Unfortunately for me, a White police officer was hiding out of sight, and caught me in the act. The 'F word' (f_ _k) rang through my head. The officer waved me over to move towards him. "Turn around" he said and slapped the cuffs on my hands behind my back. At the time, police officers had a small office in the subway. He grabbed my arm and walked me towards the room. My mind was racing because I knew—Black boy, White cop, tucked away in a small room, out of sight from the public eye—is a really bad combination. The fear was palpable and real. My heart was thumping against the wall of my chest. I was surprised the cop could not hear it. Anything could go wrong, and if s_ _t went down, my words against his would never hold up. I thought of my mother. Ooh, she would have been pissed if she knew what I had done. I had to take what was coming to me and hold out at all costs.

When I entered the room, there were three other White officers there. "Fu_k me!", I thought. This was not good. "Hey boys, look what we got here. This one didn't think he had to pay at the turnstile like everyone else," he said with a slight grin and chuckle. The arresting officer sat me down in a chair with my hands still handcuffed behind my back and said, "What's your name? Where do you live?" his face only a few inches from mine. The way he asked the question and the tone he used made me feel like I was in for a long night. I did not give him an answer, in fear of him calling my mother. "Why did you jump the turnstile?" he asked again. "I don't know," I said. That was a truthful answer, because, like I said before, I really did not know why I did it. The interrogation went on for a few more minutes without me capitulating and giving up the information he wanted. Suddenly, the door opened, and a Black police officer walked into the room. A feeling of relief, safety and calm swept over me. The words, "Thank you Lord Jesus," rang like a mantra through my mind. The White officer filled in the Black officer what I had done. The Black officer then walked over to me and resumed the interrogation. "Where are you from? Where do you live?" he asked. I did not answer, and then out of nowhere, he swung his fist and punched me as hard as he could in the middle of my chest. I crumpled over in pain, like discarded tin foil, but I still did not answer him. I felt a sense of betrayal by this Black police officer. These words flashed across my mind, "this dude may be worse than them." Eventually, after a few more minutes of back and forth, I got off with a warning and promised to never to do it again and was released.

My mother never learned of this incident, and I never jumped the turnstile again or ran afoul of the law. I was taught two lessons that day. The first was, do not break the law. The second was, that Black officers are to be feared like White officers and are no friends of Black citizens, because they have been co-opted by a cruel and unjust system. Co-optation is "the act or process of being assimilated or taken over by a larger or more established group."[75] A good example of this is the highly publicized case of five Black police officers who beat and killed Tyre Nichols, a Black man.[76] These Black officers are good examples of law enforcement officers who can easily lose themselves in the process of co-optation and follow the code of the "thin blue line."

I recently read the story of Stephens, who at the time was an 18-year-old Black boy hanging out with the wrong crowd. Two of the unsavory characters that Stephens was hanging out with were Nolen, another Black 17-year-old boy, and Melendres, a White 29-year-old man. Melendres, somehow, convinced Stephens and Nolen to do a home invasion with him using a gun. All three perpetrators were eventually caught, arrested, and convicted for the home invasion crime they committed. In the sentencing phase of the courtroom trial, the judge sentenced Stephens to 1,823 years, Nolen to 33 years, and the lone White defendant, Melendres, to 10 years, all for the same home invasion charge. This is a clear example why the blood of people of color boils at the corrupt, racist, and arbitrary application of the law.[77] There is a long history of collusion between police departments, district attorneys, and judges.[78] A corrupt cesspool that consciously or unconsciously targets Black and Brown people. It is the very reason parents of color counsel their children to walk the straight and narrow to avoid falling prey to a corrupt system, infused with White supremacy.

American culture was built on a steady diet of hate. John Blake, a CNN reporter, suggested we may never find a vaccine for the fear that White people have of encountering Black men in public spaces.[79] This virus is firmly entrenched in American culture and has metastasized throughout the media and institutions, which sadly is our reality now. The con, since the dawn of the slave era, was to convince White Americans that most Black and Brown people are to be feared, that they are criminals, and deserve to be locked up. Fast-forward to twenty-first-century America, the practice of criminalizing Black and Brown children at an early age persists. As the U.S. Government Accountability Office points out, Black children represent 15.5% of all public-school students but represent 39% of students suspended from school.[80] According to the National Prevention Science Coalition to Improve Lives, racial disparities with respect to suspension appear as early as preschool.[81] Black children represent only 19% of preschool students in the nation, yet they account for 47% of preschool children receiving more than one out-of-school suspension.[82]

FIGURE 6. Criminalization of Black boys. Source: Facebook

In figure 6, two elementary school boys are put in handcuffs in Troy, New York when they "fit the description" for a robbery. When the police realized they were wrong, the officers released the boys and joked to each other that they could still arrest them for jaywalking.[83] I ask, which White community or parent would this behavior be acceptable to, if this were happening in your community or to your own children? Laura Abrams argued that at every conceivable stage, there is an increase and overrepresentation of Black youth relative to White youth in the juvenile justice system.[84] Keith Smolkowski found that even when they controlled for poverty, participation in gifted-and-talented programs, student-teacher ratio, attendance rates, and other factors, African American students were still disciplined at higher rates and more severely than White students.[85] White students' behavior, in contrast, is often dismissed with little to no consequences. How does one account for this?

The majority of Americans believe the United States judicial systems is broken and in dire need of reform.[86] For me, and perhaps for most Black and Brown Americans, the judicial system is a horror show, stacked with White judges who seemingly are willing to dish out lengthy sentences to Black and Brown people, while showing leniency to those who are of the same race as them. As the United States Sentencing Commission recently acknowledged, "Black men statistically received harsher prison sentences than White men who commit the same crimes."[87] A public defender in Northern Virginia, Brad Haywood, who lives, breathes and witnessed the machinations of the court system, states that "the simple answer is racism… It's no shock to me that somebody who's Black goes into a courtroom and isn't given the fair shake that somebody who's White gets."[88] Just digest this fact for a minute. Eighty percent of people sentenced under the three-strikes law in California are people of color: "*Leandro Andrade* was sentenced to 50 years to life for stealing $153 worth of videotapes. *Curtis Wilkerson* was sentenced to 25 years to life for stealing a pair of socks. *Allan McIntosh* similarly received a 25-to-life sentence when he was found with a weapon after being stopped by police for riding his bike with a broken light and not using the crosswalk. *Vincent Rico* went to prison for life for stealing two pairs of kid's shoes."[89]

The Sentencing Project, a Washington D.C. based organization that advocates for unjustly incarcerated people, "found cracks in the American criminal justice system that can allow inherent biases of judges and prosecutors to influence the severity of charges and length of punishments for Black and Brown people compared to Whites who commit the same crimes."[90] As Stephanie Morales, a Portsmouth Commonwealth Attorney further states, "Our systems of power have been rooted in racism from their inception …We have system actors who are in positions of power like myself, prosecutors, judges, police officers, who won't admit that, and largely that is a part of the problem."[91] Nefarious actors in the American judicial system are plentiful and the facts are irrefutable in light of the sheer numbers. Ella Wiley, a senior communications associate at the Legal Defense Fund argues how American courtrooms are producing wrongful convictions and mass incarceration, some of which are blatantly intentional.[92] Wiley singles out in particular the infamous misconduct of Mississippi District Attorney, Doug Evans:

> In one of the most egregious and infamous examples of this kind of systemic discrimination, former Mississippi District Attorney Doug Evans struck Black jurors *4.4 times more frequently* than White jurors over the course of his nearly 30-year career. Under Evans' authority, defendant Curtis Flowers, who is Black, faced six trials for the same charge, each resulting in a hung jury or a reversed conviction due to prosecutorial misconduct. During those six trials, Evans removed 41 of 42 potential Black jurors and struck them 20 times more frequently than White jurors.

> When Flowers' case was brought to the Supreme Court, LDF filed an *amicus brief* condemning the exclusion of Black Americans from a crucial part of the democratic process. In 2019, the Supreme Court *reversed* Flowers' conviction and condemned Evans' use of racist peremptory strikes, instituting protections against striking potential jurors based on race.

> "The Flowers story is a powerful reminder that discrimination is alive and well in the criminal legal system right now. We cannot pretend it's some sort of unfortunate chapter from American history that we've now moved beyond," remarks LDF Deputy Director of Litigation Chris Kemmitt. "It continues to pervade

our criminal legal system—and not just implicit bias, but open, naked racism."[93]

Controlling the Movement of Black and Brown Bodies in Public Spaces

Misdemeanor laws such as jaywalking, loitering or trespassing have been used historically to control the movement of Black and Brown people in public spaces, which often leads to unintended consequences, such as legal fees, incarceration, or even death.[94] George Zimmerman, who shot and killed the Floridian Black youth Trayvon Martin in 2012, was instructed by a police dispatcher not to get out of his car to confront Trayvon. When Mr. Zimmerman ignored the police dispatcher's instructions, he was the aggressor who created the situation that led to Trayvon's death.[95] This country is skilled at marketing aggression to look like self-defense, often at the expense of people of color.

According to a recent documentary, *Racially Charged*, produced by Brave New Film, misdemeanor laws emanated from the South, where legislators criminalized walking next to a railroad, even in an era where no sidewalk existed.[96] No stretch of imagination is required to know who these jaywalking laws were primarily intended to prosecute and were enforced against. According to Brave

New Films, "89% of New York City jaywalk tickets are issued to Black and Brown people; 95% of Ferguson, MO jaywalking tickets are issued to Black and Brown people; and 91% of Urbana, IL jaywalk tickets are issued to Black and Brown people".[97] As Gaye Theresa Johnson, Associate Professor of Chicano and African American Studies at UCLA, further argues, "Misdemeanors are a very specific mechanism that legalize violence towards Black people and keep them in a very particular place, not just as an individual but as an entire community of people."[98]

In a highly publicized 2018 national case, two African American men were singled out by a Starbucks employee for trespassing, when they were just there to meet a business associate for coffee like any other customer in the store.[99] This illustrates the lengths to which some White people are willing to intentionally flex their privilege to control Black and Brown people in public spaces. In an interview with a CNN reporter, a White patron, Melissa DePino, who was at the Starbucks at the time of the incident, implied that this does not happen to White people. DePino quoted an outraged customer who witnessed everything who said, "I am sitting here with my Gatorade, and I have been here for two hours, and nobody says anything to me…. I had mentioned that I had been there, in that store, the day before, and I sat there for an hour, and I didn't order anything. I was waiting for my son, and then I left."[100]

The systemic double standard applied throughout American society to people of color, when compared to the White privileged class, could not be clearer. There are two Americas with respect to how American laws are enforced and applied. As Irene Oritseweyinmi Joe, a professor at the UC-Davis School of Law, argues, "Black people charged with a misdemeanor are 75% more likely to be locked up than White people".[101] Controlling Black and Brown bodies in public spaces is not limited to law enforcement. People of color are also unwelcome in some predominantly White public spaces. Take the highly publicized case of Ahmaud Aubery. Ahmaud was a 25 year-old African American man who was chased, cornered, shot, and killed by three White men for jogging through a White South Georgia neighborhood.[102]

One could argue that the arbitrary and unilateral enforcement of misdemeanor laws like jaywalking, loitering, and trespassing of people of color, is Jim Crow 2.0, seemingly designed to inhibit the movement of Black and Brown people. How else can one explain why an average of 91% of misdemeanor tickets, like jaywalking, are issued in some states to Black and Brown people when they comprise a small percentage of the population?[103]

Financial Cost of Misdemeanor Laws for People of Color

As noted earlier, misdemeanor laws like jaywalking, loitering, trespassing and traffic infractions have been used historically by police to unjustly stop Black and Brown people. A police officer can arbitrarily stop a person of color at their discretion, and if that person resists, they can be ticketed and arrested on misdemeanor charges, which stays on their record permanently and fines could take years to pay off. According to Brave New Films, "Nationwide, almost 9,000 statutes disqualify people with misdemeanors from jobs, housing, education, and other core needs,"[104] which disproportionately affects poor Black and Brown Americans who cannot afford these fees. This in not only unreasonable and unethical, but further exposes the ruthless obsession and utter disdain White America has for Black and Brown people. As Alexandra Natapoff, a professor at the Harvard Law School states, "The biggest misconception about misdemeanors is that they are minor,"[105] while Gaye Johnson succinctly addresses the full impact of misdemeanor fines on the poor: "Not enough people talk about what it means to have a misdemeanor on your record. It can determine the kind of job you get, to the kind of housing you can qualify for, to the kind of schools you can afford to go to. A lot of people are harmed for life because of the smallest infractions."[106]

From the first day African slaves were brought onto the shores of Jamestown, VA, they were forced to provide free labor and generated untold wealth for White elites. Today, White American elites continue to economically saddle the backs of poor Black and Brown people with misdemeanor crimes, which have had limited to no impact on society as a whole but provide an unending supply of economic wealth for states.[107] As Paul Delano Butler, a professor at Georgetown University's Law Center states, "Misdemeanors … have almost nothing to do with public safety. What misdemeanors do is give police an extraordinary amount of discretion with any minor offense, premised on the idea that the Black man is a threat."[108] Monica Llorente further reports on how court fines, fees, and costs have criminalized poverty by burying people with mounting debts and imposing severe punishments on them for failure to pay.[109]

Blue Collar Versus White Collar Criminals

Arguably, white-collar crimes may have a greater negative impact on American society than blue-collar crimes. The con has been propagated for decades by the media and politicians, which is to sell to the American people the ills of blue-collar crimes perpetrated by society's lower class, Black and Brown people. The false argument is that white-collar crime is "victimless" or that it only harms corporations and wealthy individuals, and therefore it is less harmful to society compared to blue-collar crime, which is often seen as more violent and impacting individuals more directly.[110] For argument's sake, let us contrast how the United States criminal justice system handles white-collar criminals, who are predominantly White Americans, and perhaps commit greater economic harm to American society than Black and Brown convicted criminals. It is estimated that white-collar crimes, meaning crimes such as bank fraud, embezzlement, and Ponzi schemes, cost an estimated $1 trillion per year, while blue-collar crimes cost only $15 billion per year.[111]

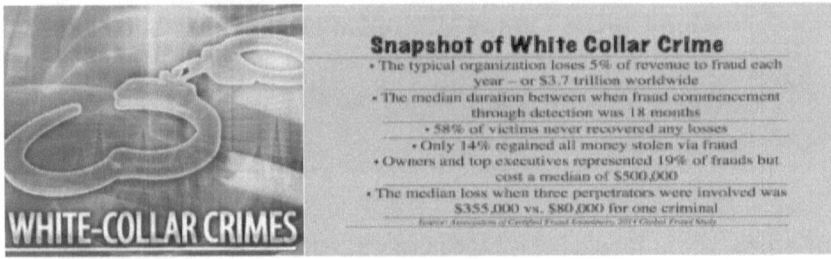

FIGURE 7. White-Collar Crimes. Source: Enterprise AI[112]

Take the case of Reed Slatkin, one of the founders of the internet service provider, EarthLink. Slatkin allegedly fleeced an estimated 850 investors to the tune of $600 million.[113] Slatkin's fraud included fleecing investors of their business profits, college funds, and retirement money. He only served 10 years for this fraudulent scheme. This misperception about white-collar crime can have significant and widespread impacts on society, including financial harm to individuals, economic instability, and loss of trust in institutions. Judges and federal attorney generals seemingly are less inclined to prosecute white-collar crimes, which are predominantly committed by White men, while going all out to prosecute and imprison Black and Brown people for blue-collar crimes. This speaks to the racial injustice that continues to exist in the American judicial system.[114]

The American justice system cannot deem itself to be impartial or just, when such racist practices are still prevalent when dispensing out inequitable sentences to Black and Brown people. The American scale of justice tilts grossly in favor of those of White skin, yet it is expected those who bear its wretched distortion of justice to recognize and honor the very people who lock them up with the unearned title of "Your Honor." Honor is earned when justice is dispensed justly, devoid of bias. As Dr. Melanie Killen, a University of Maryland psychologist deftly claims, "Everyone holds biases of one kind or another ... Maybe we can't eliminate them, but we can do all we can to avoid acting on them."[115]

We live in a constant climate of hate, intentionally aimed at Black and Brown bodies by those in power who do not share our skin complexion. If our screams are irritable and loud, America, it is only because your muted indifference has been deaf to our cries, or worse, was preoccupied with sustaining the privileged ones. We demand the same safety net for our children, which your sons and daughters peacefully sleep under. Tyranny and justice cannot coexist on the battlefield, for one will inevitably supplant the other. Thus, if you are a friend of justice, demand it for all Americans.

Chapter V

When you are accustomed to privilege, equality feels like oppression.

–Unknown[116a]

How AmeriCAN Change

While the alleged biological foundations of White supremacy, such as craniometry, have been proven as false pseudo-science by the scientific community, AmeriCon has been a part of the American fabric since the birth of America.[116] The collateral damage of the AmeriCon has left the oppressed still reliant on its oppressor. For too long, my Black and Brown people have been shaped by their oppressor on how to see themselves. They do not see themselves in their own likeness, but that of the oppressor's ancestral heritage. The time has come for the oppressed to reclaim their dignity and embrace their own ancestral likeness and history, to make whole their collective psychology. A stolen legacy can be found again. We cannot ask the White man to change and embrace our history, if we do not first relearn how to love the images we see in the mirror and the beauty of our historical past.

White supremacy has historically been promoted through institutions, customs, and beliefs that make up America's power culture, which influences its political and social landscape. Since the birth of America, White supremacy has manifested itself through slavery, Jim Crow laws, a segregated and unequal education system, political disenfranchisement, and housing discrimination. The political and economic structures of the United States, as well as the power culture that supports them, have contributed significantly to the persistence of White supremacy by enabling White citizens to enjoy power, privilege, and control of Black and Brown bodies. Dining at the table of privilege, conditions the palate of the ruling class to endlessly salivate for unearned entitlements, seemingly, for no other reasons than the melanin they possess. They never question why they have these entitlements and others do not. What we do know is these entitlements provide huge benefits to the ruling class when it comes to the application of jobs, criminal justice, policing, housing, education, and finance.

An example of this was in the 1930s, when the federal government passed the New Deal, which was a set of policies implemented to aid Americans in their recovery from the Great

Depression. The New Deal gave many White Americans much-needed relief, but it left Black and Brown people out of many of its advantages.[117] By refusing to insure mortgages for people of color, the Federal Housing Administration (FHA) effectively prevented them from purchasing homes and accumulating wealth.[118] These intentional actions maintained White citizens' privilege and power at the expense of Black and Brown citizens, which significantly contributed to the continuation of White hegemony. Americas' racist past must be acknowledged and confronted to build a society that is more just and equal for everyone.

Eradicating White hegemony necessitates a multidimensional strategy that includes education, systemic change, taking action, accountability, and self-reflection. It will be hard work to change, but it is essential for creating a more just and equitable society for all Americans. To change these privileged practices, a long-term, concerted action from individuals, communities, and organizations at all levels of society is required. Education must be at the top of the list to educate and expose the origins of White supremacy, its effects on communities of color, and methods of sustaining it through institutions. Systemic racism, which is deeply rooted in institutions and policies, is what keeps White hegemony alive. Examining the practices and policies in institutions that uphold White supremacy and changing them to build a more equal and just society, is necessary to end systemic racism. This includes addressing problems like the *school-to-prison pipeline* that overwhelmingly affects students of color, "which refers to education and public safety policies that push students into the criminal legal system. Schools send students into the pipeline through zero-tolerance disciplinary policies, which involve the police in minor misbehavior and often lead to arrests and juvenile detention referrals",[119a] and *redlining*, which is "a discriminatory practice that consists of the systematic denial of services such as mortgages, insurance loans, and other financial services to residents of certain areas, based on their race or ethnicity".[119b] This may require participating in neighborhood-based initiatives to advance justice and equity in one's community. Holding people accountable, for example, by exposing and opposing racist speech and behavior, as well as supporting sanctions against those who harbor and act upon racist views and contribute to the perpetuation of White supremacy, includes demanding accountability from public officials, such as politicians, for their actions and remarks. Lastly, self-reflecting is also a requisite for examining one's attitudes and deeds, identify and combat one's own biases and privilege, as well promoting one's own education and growth.

Twenty-First Century Media in the Lead

Through the centuries, the American media has played a prominent role promoting White supremacy through negative images and racist language. The American media often fosters a narrative that negatively portrays people of color as inferior or dangerous through racist caricatures. Collette Watson recounts how the media impacted her in New York with respect to Black and Brown people and how it still continues today:

> Growing up in Brooklyn in the 1980s, I remember how Trump was part of amplifying this media misrepresentation of Black youth that led to the conviction of five Black kids [the Central Park Five]. He put out a full-page newspaper ad calling for their deaths, and he could do that—because he was rich, he was White, and he was a man.
>
> I remember the language of that time: 'Crack baby. AIDS patient. Super-predator. Welfare mom.' And how all of these portrayals became part of this official story with books like *The Bell Curve* and others that told the story of our inferiority.
>
> This is the '80s and the '90s. Not the '50s, the '30s and the '20s … not the 1800s. This is just a few years ago, within my lifetime. And it's happening today. Our media system is the same as any

other system in this country: It wasn't created to help Black folks; it was created to harm Black folks. From the first continuous newspaper to the present day, the media system has worked to uphold a white-racial hierarchy. Its goal has always been to create a myth of Black inferiority. Narratives are a political tool that have been weaponized to harm Black and Indigenous folks and other people of color."[119]

In the nineteenth and twentieth centuries, Black people were regularly portrayed in newspapers and other media outlets as being lazy, illiterate, and criminal.[120] These representations helped to legitimize systematic racism, including segregation and discrimination, by reinforcing negative preconceptions. Furthermore, the media frequently portrayed people of color, as, in some way, "different." This promotes and fosters a feeling of otherness, which can result in prejudice and violence.

To be clear, the underrepresentation of people of color in the media, by default, promotes White hegemony, because there is no filter to keep White people in check when they are making biased decisions on matters of race. The idea that people of color are less significant or less deserving of attention than White people is reinforced when they are either absent from or only sparingly and stereotypically featured in the media. When Black and Brown people are underrepresented in the media, it is easier for White people to discount or reject their experiences and viewpoints, which may contribute to the persistence of systemic racism. Therefore, it is crucial to encourage diversity and inclusion in the media to counteract racial stereotype imagery that reinforces White supremacy. Boosting the presence of Black and Brown people in mainstream media, ensures that they are accurately and respectfully portrayed. The sea change that must happen in America's media and newsrooms is the racial and ethnic diversification of editors, writers, producers, and executive producers.

Some media organizations have begun to recognize the complicit role they played to advance White supremacy and the indoctrination of the American public. In a 2018 dedicated memorial ceremony to the thousands of past lynched victims, the *Montgomery Advertiser* (Alabama) apologized for its coverage of African American murders from the 1870s to the 1950s.[121] In an act of contrition, in a front page-editorial, the Board stated, "we were wrong and careless in reporting during that period…. We propagated a world view rooted in racism and the sickening myth of racial superiority."[122]

The media can play a pivotal role in ending White supremacy because it has an undeniable influence on how the public views and feels about race: The media can aid in the promotion of more inclusive and equitable narratives about race by taking steps to diversity representation, confront damaging stereotypes, offer context and historical perspective, elevate diverse viewpoints, and hold themselves accountable. These steps include: (1) Diversify representation to include a wider range of perspectives in their reporting. This means expanding the number of people of color working in newsrooms and making sure that all forms of media accurately and respectfully portray people of color. This can aid in dispelling negative stereotypes and fostering more favorable views of Black and Brown people. (2) Criticize racist language and imagery by an outright critique of objectionable material. This means, encouraging more courteous and impartial language in news reports as well as actively combating damaging stereotypes in the entertainment industry. Furthermore, while covering news involving racial concerns, media outlets should be mindful not to use provocative and sensational language. (3) Provide context and historical perspective to help people better comprehend racial-related issues. Promote diversified voices that provide different perspectives and viewpoints from underrepresented groups on racial issues and commit to performing internal accountability to reflect on the role they played in sustaining White supremacy and implement policies to change those behavioral practices. This means admitting previous errors and resolving to report the news equitably and fairly on matters of race.

An Inclusive Educational System

The American education system is not inclusive and has a long history of excluding people of color. This exclusion started with slavery, when those who were enslaved were forbidden from receiving an education, and it continued with segregation and discriminatory laws that forbade Black and Brown people from enrolling in well-funded institutions of higher education.[123] Many schools in low-income communities of color are still underfunded and neglected today, which results in a shortage of supplies, inferior facilities, and poor instruction.[124] The manifestations of this exclusion are represented in textbooks and curricula, where the contributions and viewpoints of people of color are omitted in the classroom. By encouraging a history and culture that is centered on

White people and neglecting or underplaying the experiences and contributions of people of color, this exclusion, by default, passively promotes White supremacy.

There are many steps that can be taken to incorporate people of color in the American education system: (1) We can begin with expanding access to high-quality education to marginalized populations. This includes ensuring that schools in low-income areas have access to sufficient supplies, infrastructure, and trained instructors, and diversifying the curriculum and teaching methods to ensure the historical contributions and viewpoints of people of color are taught in American schools. This means to ensure that textbooks and other educational materials appropriately depict the experiences of people of color, promoting a more inclusive vision of history and culture, and aggressively combating damaging stereotypes and racist ideas. (2) Encourage cultural competency by giving school administrators and instructors resources and training, namely, teaching teachers about the viewpoints and experiences of people of color as well as assisting them in acquiring the abilities and expertise necessary to successfully instruct a diverse student body. (3) Lastly, promote a sense of community by making a friendly and inclusive atmosphere for all students. This means encouraging diversity and inclusion in educational policies and procedures, backing student-led diversity initiatives, and fostering interactions and mutual learning among students from various backgrounds.

Changing the American Criminal Justice System

Let's face it. The American criminal justice system is not a friend to Black and Brown people. For too long, American institutions have played the role of blockers of justice, equity, and inclusion when it comes to people of color's rights and freedom to live freely and realize the American dream. Racial profiling, excessive policing of communities of color, unequal treatment in the judicial system, and the maintenance of harmful stereotypes and racist views are just a few examples of the targeting and systematic racism that goes on in the criminal justice system.

Racial profiling is one of the most prevalent ways that the criminal justice system uses to single out people of color for special treatment. Black and Brown people have been complaining for decades of this discriminatory practice that disproportionately targets people of color. This pattern of over-policing communities of color often leads to the arrest of Black and Brown citizens for trivial matters, such as jaywalking, "stop-and-frisk," illegal search and seizure, and request for their identification without any crimes being committed.[125] These inequitable treatments often result in unlawful detainment, arrest, incarceration, and unjust sentencing. This unjust treatment further feeds the racial inequality cycle and encourages the notion that people of color are less deserving of justice. The continuation of these bad policies and stereotypes helps foster a racist belief that fuels and maintains this corrupt criminal justice system.

Actionable steps are needed to change the American criminal justice system and how it polices Black and Brown communities. To promote a more inclusive and equitable criminal justice system, policies and laws need to change, and continual education around fairness and justice must be sustained. The American criminal justice system can take several actions to stop these discriminatory practices by putting in place regulations and procedures that forbid the use of prejudicial policies like "stop-and-frisk." These kinds of policies would never be acceptable in White communities, nor would they survive legal scrutiny. The question is, why are these practices acceptable in Black and Brown communities?

To eradicate these discriminatory practices, we need a more comprehensive strategy that addresses and incorporates laws and procedures to end racial profiling, encourage community-based policing, boost accountability and transparency, encourage restorative justice, address racial disparities in sentencing, and confront damaging stereotypes among its rank and file. Communities of color need to be protected by outlawing racial profiling practices like "stop-and-frisk," illegal search and seizures, and putting in place training programs to inform law-enforcement personnel on the negative effects of these practices. Positive community-based policing is a good way for the police to build trust with the local communities they serve. This may involve providing training programs that inform officers on the value of community engagement and funding community policing initiatives that foster relationships between law enforcement and communities.

Law Enforcement Accountability and Transparency

One of the biggest challenges for law enforcement is actively combating and weeding out racist officers among the rank-and-file police force. This needs to be a top priority for law enforcement leadership. This means creating a culture that exposes racist behavior and rewards police officers willing to come forth with the information. Furthermore, training courses that inform police about the negative effects of racism and prejudice on the department, as well as opening up channels of communication and engagement between law enforcement and communities of color should be at the top of the priority list. Another glaring problem with law enforcement and the communities they serve is a lack of trust and their unwillingness to share their crime data.[126] Improving law enforcement accountability and transparency will be central to improving community trust. Law enforcement must document, collect, and disseminate data on policing activities, such as arrest rates, use of force events, and disciplinary proceedings to improve accountability and openness, especially with the minority communities they serve.

AmeriCAN

Diversity, equity, and inclusion are not expressly mentioned in the U.S. Constitution. However, these ideas are covered by a number of amendments and legal precedents. The Equal Protection Clause of the United States Constitution's Fourteenth Amendment, passed in 1868, states that no state shall "deny to any person within its jurisdiction the equal protection of the laws."[127] In other words, all Americans should be treated equally under the law regardless of color, ethnicity, religion, or gender. There are also a number of government regulations in place that support diversity, equity, and inclusion in a variety of societal contexts, including work, education, and housing. For instance, the Fair Housing Act of 1968 forbids discrimination in housing based on race, color, religion, sex, or national origin, and Title VII of the Civil Rights Act of 1964 bars discrimination in employment on identical grounds.[128]

Americans can do better by creating a world where systemic injustice no longer thrives and is replaced with a bubbling world of opportunity where diversity, equity, and inclusion are embraced as cornerstones of American justice. This calls for a readiness to actively oppose and destroy oppressive structures as well as a commitment to continued learning and development relating to problems of equality and justice. This means actively seeking out opportunities to learn about the struggles faced by oppressed communities, combating personal preconceptions and biases in our own attitudes and behaviors, conversing with people from different racial backgrounds, lobbying for legislative changes and reforms that advance equality and justice, and attempting to gain a deeper comprehension of the underlying factors that lead to systematic injustice.

Americans can create a better America. Instead of looking to others to make a change, *you* be the change by making your actions at work inclusive of others. Make your neighborhoods safe and welcoming to people who look different from you. Strive to advance equality and justice in your own social circle.

In America, the White man is known as American while all other races are hyphenated by race- Native American, African American, or Mexican American in history books, media, newspapers, schools, and government institutions. Maybe the day will come when the need to address each other by race will no longer be necessary. Just Americans will do.

To the other America: our days are long, our nights even longer, but remain resolute, for the light of hope shines brilliantly over the horizon. Our journey is tasked with fulfilling the American dream, a reality rooted in fairness and justice for all. We must fulfill the duty that was mandated by our forefathers. AmeriCAN!

Notes

1. German Lopez, "A Lasting Impact: 'The 1619 Project' Continues to Provoke National Debate about Race and History," *The New York Times*, January 26, 2003, https://www.nytimes.com/2023/01/26/briefing/the-1619-project-hulu-show.html

Austin J. Pickup & Aubrey Brammar Southall, "A Critical Discourse Analysis of the 1619 Project Controversy and Its Implications for Social Studies Educators," *The Social Studies*, 113:5, 223-236, DOI 10.1080/00377996.2022.2039892

2. Lopez, "A Lasting Impact."

3. "A Journey in Chain," Library of Congress, accessed October 31, 2023, page 2. https://www.loc.gov/classroom-materials/immigration/african/journey-in-chains/

4. Library of Congress, "A Journey in Chains," page 2.

5. Faisal Shah, "A System is a Collection of Elements or Components that are Organized for a Common Purpose," *Scribd*, October 31, 2023, page 1, https://www.scribd.com/document/161380682/a-system-is-a-collection-of-elements-or-components-that-are-organized-for-a-common-purpose; "What is a System?" Future Learn, accessed October 31, 2023, https://www.futurelearn.com/info/courses/understanding-systems-thinking-in-healthcare/0/steps/76298

Malcolm W. Hoag, "Letter To The Editor- What Is A System?" *Operations Research*, 1957 5:3, 445-447, https://pubsonline.informs.org/doi/epdf/10.1287/opre.5.3.445

6. Courtland Milloy, "How American Oligarchs Created the Concept of Race to Divide and Conquer the Poor," *Washington Post*, April 19, 2016. https://www.washingtonpost.com/local/how-wealthy-americans-divided-and-conquered-the-poor-to-create-the-concept-of-race/2016/04/19/2cab6e38-0643-11e6-b283-e79d81c63c1b_story.html

Jeffery A. Winters, "OLIGARCHY IN THE U.S.A.," *In these Times*, *36*, 16-20, 5, https://go.openathens.net/redirector/liberty.edu?url=https://www.pro quest.com/magazines/oligarchy-u-s/docview/925799024/se-2

7. Nikole Hannah-Jones, "Our Democracy's Founding Ideals Were False When They Were Written. Black Americans Have Fought to Make Them True," *The New York Times*, August 14, 2019, https://www.nytimes.com/interactive/2019/08/14/magazine/black-history-american-democracy.html

8. Hannah-Jones, "Our Democracy's Founding Ideals Were False When They Were Written," page 4.

8-a. "Demographics of Jamaica," *Wikipedia*, 2022, https://en.wikipedia.org/wiki/Demographics_of_Jamaica#Population

9. Alexandria Miller, "Jamaican Independence," *Origins,* August, 2022, https://origins.osu.edu/read/jamaican-independence?language_content_entity=en

[9a] "The Philosophy of Colonialism: Civilization, Christianity, and Commerce," *Scholar Blogs*, 2016, https://scholarblogs.emory.edu/violenceinafrica/sample-page/the-philosophy-of-colonialism-civilization-christianity-and-commerce/

[9b]9 "The Philosophy of Colonialism," *Scholar Blogs*.

10. "The Philosophy of Colonialism," *Scholar Blogs*.

[11a] The Historian 13, "Phil from Modern *Family*- "If you ain't White, you ain't right". *Youtube*. Video Length: 0:42, Run Time: 0:15-0:42, https://www.youtube.com/watch?v=CzgDmqGnQDk

11. Kaleigh Howland, "Fleming: Media Plays Role in White Supremacy," *The Media School*, Indiana University Bloomington,October 12, 2018, https://mediaschool.indiana.edu/news-events/news/item.html?n=fleming-media-plays-role-in-white-supremacy

Mohammed el-Nawawy & Mohamad Hamas Elmasry, "White Supremacy on CNN and Fox: AC 360 and Hannity Coverage of the Charlottesville 'Unite the Right' Rally," *Journalism Practice*, 17:5, 948-969, DOI 10.1080/17512786.2021.1967187

12. Cambridge Dictionary, "Con," *DictionaryCambrige.org*, accessed October 31, 2023, https://dictionary.cambridge.org/us/dictionary/english/con?q=con-

13. Michael T. Rizzo, Tobias C. Britton, and Marjorie Thodes, "Developmental Origins of Anti-Black Bias in White Children in the United States: Exposure to and Beliefs about Racial Inequality," *Psychological and Cognitive Sciences* 119, no. 47 (2022): e2209129119, https://www.pnas.org/doi/10.1073/pnas.2209129119

14. Rizzo, Britton, and Thodes, "Developmental Origins of Anti-Black Bias," p. 1

15. Rizzo, Britton, and Thodes, "Developmental Origins of Anti-Black Bias," p. 2

16. Larry Adelman, "Race: The Power of an Illusion," *PBS.org*, 2003, https://www.pbs.org/race/000_About/002_04-background-03-02.htm

17. Adelman, "Race: The Power of an Illusion," p. 1

18 .Twin Cities PBS, "Redlining and Racial Covenants: Jim Crow of the North," *YouTube video*, 2021, Video Length: 8.00. https://www.youtube.com/watch?v=ymOaiWla3DU

Perry Abello Oscar, "Breaking Through and Breaking Down the Delmar Divide in St. Louis: For generations, racial covenants and redlining devastated housing in the city's historically African-American neighborhoods north of Delmar Boulevard. Now a new mortgage program seeks to reduce hypervacancy and make homeownership feasible for residents." *Forefront,* https://go.openathens.net/redirector/liberty.edu?url=https://www.proquest.com/magazines/breaking-through-down-delmar-divide-st-louis/docview/2275917461/se-2

19. Lyrics On Demand, "Danie Boone Lyrics," TV Themes, accessed October 31, 2023, p. 1, https://www.lyricsondemand.com/tvthemes/danielboonelyrics.html

20. Tracy Jan, "How White TV Writers Decide the Stories Hollywood Tells America," *The Washington Post*, November 6, 2017, https://www.washingtonpost.com/news/wonk/wp/2017/11/06/how-white-tv-writers-shape-the-stories-hollywood-tells-america/

   Jing Yang, "The Reinvention of Hollywood's Classic White Saviour Tale in Contemporary Chinese Cinema: Pavilion of Women and The Flowers of War," *Critical Arts*, 28:2, 247-263, DOI: 10.1080/02560046.2014.906343

21. Marshall McLuhan, *Understanding Media: The Extensions of Man,* (Cambridge, Massachussets: The MIT Press, 1964).

22. Howland, "Fleming: Media Plays Role in White supremacy."

23. Howland, "Fleming: Media Plays Role in White supremacy," p. 1

24. Alicia Bell, "What Is Media 2070?" Media 2070, 2022, https://mediareparations.org/about/

25. Bell, "What Is Media 2070?" p. 1

26. Colette Watson, "How the Media System Fuels Anti-Black Racism," *Free Press*, March 8, 2021, https://www.freepress.net/blog/how-media-system-fuels-anti-black-racism

27. Watson, "How the Media System Fuels Anti-Black Racism."

28. Watson, "How the Media System Fuels Anti-Black Racism."

29. Watson, "How the Media System Fuels Anti-Black Racism." p. 1

30. Global Strategy Group, "Report Documents Racial Bias in Coverage of Crime by Media," *Equal Justice Initiative*, December 6,2021, https://eji.org/news/report-documents-racial-bias-in-coverage-of-crime-by-media/

31. Global Strategy Group, "Report Documents Racial Bias in Coverage of Crime by Media."

32. Global Strategy Group, "Report Documents Racial Bias in Coverage of Crime by Media."

33. Global Strategy Group, "Report Documents Racial Bias in Coverage of Crime by Media."

34. Jenée Desmond-Harris, "These 2 Sets of Pictures Are Everything You Need to Know about Race, Crime, and Media Bias," *Vox.com*, April 1, 2015, p. 1, https://www.vox.com/2015/4/1/8326315/media-bias-black-mughsots

35. Desmond-Harris, "These 2 Sets of Pictures Are Everything You Need to Know About Race, Crime, and Media Bias."

36. Tracy Jan, "News Media Offers Consistently Warped Portrayals of Black Families, Study Finds.," *The Washington Post*, December 13, 2017, https://www.washingtonpost.com/news/wonk/wp/2017/12/13/news-media-offers-consistently-warped-portrayals-of-black-families-study-finds/

37. Spike Lee, "Malcolm X," *Amazon Prime Video*, 1992, https://www.amazon.com/gp/video/detail/B0097JUG86/ref=atv_dp_share_cu_r

38. Yale School of Public Health. "Racialism and the Media: Stereotypes, Biased Frames, Historical Myths and Traditional Racism," *YouTube.com*, February 9, 2022, https://www.youtube.com/watch?v=mdhZGucB7ic

39. A. Clayton, "Ron DeSantis Bans African American Studies Class from Florida High Schools," *The Guardian*, January 19, 2023, https://www.theguardian.com/us-news/2023/jan/19/ron-desantis-bans-african-american-studies-florida-schools

James Fallows, "'WHAT'S THE MATTER WITH FLORIDA?':
The GOP's doomed war against higher ed." *Washington Monthly*,
ol55, no. 9-10, Sept.-Oct. 2023, pp. 20+. *Gale In Context:
Biography*,
link.gale.com/apps/doc/A763616870/BIC?u=vic_liberty&sid=summ
on&xid=628bd5dd

40. Clayton, "Ron DeSantis Bans African American Studies Class
from Florida High Schools."

"The Problem of Bias in US History Textbooks and
Curriculum," School of Education Online Programs, May 24, 2021,
https://soeonline.american.edu/blog/bias-in-history-textbooks/

41a Chelsea Bailey and Brandon Drenon, "Florida's attle Over How
Race Is Taught In Schools", *BBC News*, March 11, 2023, p. 1,
https://www.bbc.com/news/world-us-canada-64815035

41. Cynthia Greenlee, "How History Textbooks Reflect America's
Refusal to Reckon with Slavery," *Vox.com*, August 26, 2019,
https://www.vox.com/identities/2019/8/26/20829771/slavery-
textbooks-history

Bennett Brazelton, "Ethical Considerations on Representing
Slavery in Curriculum," *Radical Teacher*, *121*, 55–65,
https://doi.org/10.5195/rt.2021.830

42. Liz Mineo, "How Textbooks Taught White Supremacy," *The
Harvard Gazette*, September 4, 2020, p. 1,
https://news.harvard.edu/gazette/story/2020/09/harvard-historian-
examines-how-textbooks-taught-white-supremacy/

43. Julia McEvoy, "Rural Students of Color are Fighting Back
against Racism in Majority White Schools," *NPR*, May 24, 2022,
https://www.npr.org/2022/05/24/1101040192/rural-students-of-
color-are-fighting-back-against-racism-in-majority-white-schoo

Cady Berkel, Velma McBride Murry, Tera R. Hurt, Yi-fu Chen,
Gene H. Brody et al., "It Takes a Village: Protecting Rural African
American Youth in the Context of Racism," *Journal of Youth and
Adolescence, 38*(2), 175-88. https://doi.org/10.1007/s10964-008-
9346-z

44. Julia McEvoy, "Rural Students of Color are Fighting Back Against Racism in Majority White Schools," *NPR*, May 24, 2022, p. 1, https://www.npr.org/2022/05/24/1101040192/rural-students-of-color-are-fighting-back-against-racism-in-majority-white-schoo

45. Kirsten Weir, "Inequality at School: What's Behind the Racial Disparity in Our Education System?" *Monitor on Psychology* 47, no. 10 (2016): 42, https://www.apa.org/monitor/2016/11/cover-inequality-school

46. Howard Henderson and Jennifer W. Bourgeois, "Penalizing Black Hair in the Name of Academic Success is Undeniably Racist, Unfounded, and Against the Law," *Brookings,* February 23, 2021, https://www.brookings.edu/blog/how-we-rise/2021/02/23/penalizing-black-hair-in-the-name-of-academic-success-is-undeniably-racist-unfounded-and-against-the-law/

47. Carrie Spector, "How Unequal Discipline Hurts Black Students," *Greater Good Magazine*, February 6, 2020, https://greatergood.berkeley.edu/article/item/how_unequal_disciplin e_hurts_black_students

Michael Rocque and Raymond Paternoster, "Understanding the Antecedents of The 'School-To-Jail' link: The Relationship Between Race and School Discipline." *Journal of Criminal Law and Criminology*, Nov. 3 2023, vol. 101, no. 2, spring 2011, pp. 633+. *Gale OneFile: LegalTrac*,link.gale.com/apps/doc/A256777964/LT?u=vic_liberty&s id=summon&xid=edc7bb82

48. Spector, "How Unequal Discipline Hurts Black Students."

49. John Rosales and Tim Walker, "The Racist Beginnings of Standardized Testing," *NEA Today,* March 20, 2021, https://www.nea.org/advocating-for-change/new-from-nea/racist-beginnings-standardized-testing

Sevan G. Terzian, "Subtle, Vicious Effects": Lillian Steele Proctor's Pioneering Investigation of Gifted African American Children in Washington, D. C.," *History of Education Quarterly,* August 2, 2021, *61*(3), 351-371, https://doi.org/10.1017/heq.2021.22

50. Ailsa Chang and Jonaki Mehta, "Why U.S. Schools Are Still Segregated—And One Idea to Help Change That," *NPR*, July 7, 2020, https://www.npr.org/sections/live-updates-protests-for-racial-justice/2020/07/07/888469809/how-funding-model-preserves-racial-segregation-in-public-schools

51. Mineo, "How Textbooks Taught White Supremacy."

52. Mineo, "How Textbooks Taught White Supremacy."

53. Rosales and Walker, "The Racist Beginnings of Standardized Testing."

54. Gil Troy, "The Racist Origins of the SAT," *The Dailey Beast*, December 2, 2017, https://www.thedailybeast.com/author/gil-troy

Rosales and Walker, "The Racist Beginnings of Standardized Testing."

55. Teachers College, "The Color Blind Society: Whiteness as the Default Standard," *Teachers College Columbia University*, September, 2003, https://www.tc.columbia.edu/articles/2003/september/the-color-blind-society-whiteness-as-the-default-standard/

56. Rosales and Walker, "The Racist Beginnings of Standardized Testing."

57. Rosales and Walker, "The Racist Beginnings of Standardized Testing," p. 1

58. Calvin John Smiley and David Fakunle, "From 'Brute' to 'Thug:' The Demonization and Criminalization of Unarmed Black Male Victims in America," *Journal of Human Behavioral Social Environment* 26, no. 3-4 (2016): 350-366, http://doi.org/10.1080/10911359.2015.1129256

59. Li Wang, "Sociocultural Learning Theories and Information Literacy Teaching Activities in Higher Education," *Reference & User Services Quarterly* 47, no. 2 (2007): 149–158, https://doi.org/10.5860/rusq.47n2.149

60. Nicole R. Holliday and Lauren Squires, "Sociolinguistic Labor, Linguistic Climate, and Race(ism) on Campus: Black College Students' Experiences with Language at Predominantly White Institutions," *Journal of Sociolinguistics* 25, no. 3 (2020): 418–437. https://doi.org/10.1111/josl.12438

61. Dudley Davis, "Utilizing Resilience and Persistence Strategies to Reduce African American Doctoral Attrition," *Scholars Crossing*, 2022. p. 21, https://digitalcommons.liberty.edu/doctoral/4095/

62. Chelsea Candelario, "The one Phrase You Should Probably Stop Saying to BIPOC," *Pure Wow*, August 2, 2020, https://www.purewow.com/wellness/you-speak-so-well

63. Holliday and Squires, "Sociolinguistic Labor, Linguistic Climate, and Race(ism) on Campus;" A. Baker-Bell, "Dismantling Anti-Black Linguistic Racism in English Language Arts Classrooms: Toward an Anti-Racist Black Language Pedagogy," *Theory Into Practice* 59, no. 1 (2020): 8–21, http://doi.org/10.1080/00405841.2019.1665415

64. Holliday and Squires, "Sociolinguistic Labor, Linguistic Climate, and Race(ism) on Campus;" A. Baker-Bell, "Dismantling Anti-Black Linguistic Racism in English Language Arts Classrooms: Toward an Anti-Racist Black Language Pedagogy," *Theory Into Practice* 59, no. 1 (2020): 8–21, http://doi.org/10.1080/00405841.2019.1665415

65. Emily Sullivan, "Laura Ingraham Told Lebron James to Shut Up and Dribble; He Went to the Hoop," *NPR*, Maine Public, February 19, 2018. p. 1, https://www.npr.org/sections/thetwo-way/2018/02/19/587097707/laura-ingraham-told-lebron-james-to-shutup-and-dribble-he-went-to-the-hoop

66. Sullivan, "Laura Ingraham Told Lebron James to Shut Up and Dribble." p.1

67. Brett Foran, "Jive Speak Airplane!" *YouTube.com*, 2013, https://youtu.be/RrZlWw8Di10

68. Holliday and Squires, "Sociolinguistic Labor, Linguistic Climate, and Race(ism) on Campus."

69. Morning Journal, "Jive-Talking Twin Transformers Raise Race Issues," *Morning Journal*, June 25, 2009, https://www.morningjournal.com/2009/06/25/jive-talking-twin-transformers-raise-race-issues/

70. Morning Journal, "Jive-Talking Twin Transformers Raise Race Issues."

71. Jada Vasser, "The Art of Code-Switching: How Black Students Adapt to Predominantly White Spaces," *The State News*, February 27, 2023, p. 1, https://statenews.com/article/2023/02/the-art-of-codeswitching?ct=content_open&cv=cbox_latest

Adjoa E. Kusi-Appiah, "When Code-switching Is A Requisite On Clinical Rotations," *BMJ : British Medical Journal (Online)*, July 29, 2022, *378,*https://doi.org/10.1136/bmj.o1898

72. Vasser, "The Art of Code-Switching: How Black Students Adapt to Predominantly White Spaces," p. 1

73. Lisa Bertagnoli, "Everything You Need to Know about Code Switching in the Workplace," *Builtin*, June 14, 2022, https://builtin.com/diversity-inclusion/code-switching

74. Dylan Green, "Rappers Are Rejecting Code-Switching", *DJ Booth*, April 12, 2019, https://djbooth.net/features/2019-04-11-rappers-are-rejecting-code-switching

75. "Cooptation," *Dictionary.com*, October 31, 2023, https://www.dictionary.com/browse/cooptation

Markus Holdo, "Cooptation and Non-cooptation: Elite Strategies In Response To Social Protest," *Social Movement Studies*, August 19, 2017, 18:4, 444-462, DOI: 10.1080/14742837.2019.1577133

76. Nick Valencia, Elizabeth Wolfe, and Pamela Kirkland, "5 Memphis Police Officers Charged in Deadly Beating of Tyre Nichols Allegedly Assaulted Another Man Just Three Days Before, Federal Lawsuit Says," *CNN*, February 7, 2023, https://www.cnn.com/2023/02/07/us/memphis-police-scorpion-unit-arrest-lawsuit/index.html

77. Jessica Larché, "Data Shows Black Men Receive Harsher Punishments than Whites for Same Crimes," *3WTKR*, February 21, 2022, https://www.wtkr.com/investigations/data-shows-black-men-receive-harsher-punishments-than-whites-for-same-crimes

Elizabeth Hinton, LeShae Henderson, and Cindy Reed, "An Unjust Burden: The Disparate Treatment of Black Americans in the Criminal Justice System," *Vera Institute of Justice*, May, 2018, https://www.issuelab.org/resources/30758/30758.pdf

78. Larché, "Data Shows Black Men Receive Harsher Punishments than Whites for Same Crimes."

79. J. Blake, "There's One Epidemic We May Never Find a Vaccine For: Fear of Black Men in Public Spaces," *CNN*, May 26, 2020, https://www.cnn.com/2020/05/26/us/fear-black-men-blake/index.html.

80. U.S. Government Accountability Office, "K–12 Education: Discipline Disparities for Black Students, Boys, and Students with Disabilities," *U.S. Government Accountability Office*, March 22, 2018, https://www.gao.gov/products/gao-18-258;

J. A. Coles and T. Powell, "A BlackCrit Analysis on Black Urban Youth and Suspension Disproportionality as Anti-Black Symbolic Violence," *Race Ethnicity and Education* 23, no. 1 (2020), 113–33, http://doi.org/10.1080/13613324.2019.1631778

81. National Prevention Science Coalition, "Racially Disproportionate Discipline in Early Childhood Educational Settings," *National Prevention Science Coalition*, September 16, 2000. https://www.npscoalition.org/post/racially-disproportionate-discipline-in-early-childhood-educational-settings

82. National Prevention Science Coalition, "Racially Disproportionate Discipline in Early Childhood Educational Settings."

83. S. King, "Furious," *Facebook*, 2015, https://www.facebook.com/shaunking/photos/furious-these-are-two-elementary-school-boys-who-were-put-in-handcuffs-in-troy-n/892654044106848/

84. Laura S. Abrams, Matthew L. Mizel, and Elizabeth S. Barnert, "Correction to: The Criminalization of Young Children and Overrepresentation of Black Youth in the Juvenile Justice System," *Race and Social Problems* (2021), https://doi.org/10.1007/s12552-021-09324-5

85. Keith Smolkowski, Erik J. Girvan, Kent McIntosh, Rhonda N. T. Nese, and Robert H. Horner, "Vulnerable Decision Points for Disproportionate Office Discipline Referrals: Comparisons of Discipline for African American and White Elementary School Students," *Behavioral Disorders* 41, no. 4 (2016), 178–195.

86. Open Society Foundations. "Majority of Americans Think U.S. Criminal Justice System is Broken, Ineffective; See Need for Change," *Open Society Foundation*, February 12, 2002, https://www.opensocietyfoundations.org/newsroom/majority-americans-think-us-criminal-justice-system-broken-ineffective-see-need

87. Larché, "Data Shows Black Men Receive Harsher Punishments than Whites for Same Crimes."

88. Larché, "Data Shows Black Men Receive Harsher Punishments than Whites for Same Crimes."

89. Erwin Chemerinsky, Gil Garcett, and Miriam A. Krinsky, "Op-Ed: California's 'Three Strikes' Law still Carries a Devastating Human and Financial Cost. End it Now," *Los Angeles Times*, August 12, 2022, https://www.latimes.com/opinion/story/2022-08-12/three-strikes-law-prosecutor-discretion-california-costs

90. Larché, "Data Shows Black Men Receive Harsher Punishments than Whites for Same Crimes."

91. Larché, "Data Shows Black Men Receive Harsher Punishments than Whites for Same Crimes."

92. Ella Wiley, "How Racism in the Courtroom Produces Wrongful Convictions and Mass Incarceration," *Legal Defense Fund*, July 20, 2022, https://www.naacpldf.org/judicial-process-failures/

93. Ella Wiley, "How Racism in the Courtroom Produces Wrongful Convictions and Mass Incarceration," Emphasis added.

94. Brave New Films, "Racially Charged: America's Misdemeanor Problem," *YouTube*, April 1, 2021, https://youtu.be/Bm2PxE0HMr4

95. André Munro, "Shooting of Trayvon Martin," *Encyclopedia Britannica*, October 31, 2023, https://www.britannica.com/event/shooting-of-trayvon-martin.

96. Brave New Films. "Racially Charged: America's Misdemeanor Problem."

97. Brave New Films. "Racially Charged: America's Misdemeanor Problem."

98. Brave New Films. "Racially Charged: America's Misdemeanor Problem."

99. Matt Stevens, "Starbucks C.E.O. Apologizes after Arrests of 2 Black Men," *The New York Times*, April 15, 2018, https://www.nytimes.com/2018/04/15/us/starbucks-philadelphia-black-men-arrest.html

100. CNN. (2018). "Witness: This Dosen't Happen to White People," *CNN.com video*, April 17, 2028, https://www.cnn.com/videos/us/2018/04/17/philadelphia-starbucks-arrest-video-witness-depino-sot-ctn.cnn

101. Brave New Films, "Racially Charged: America's Misdemeanor Problem."

102. Richard Fausset, "What we Know about the Shooting Death of Ahmaud Arbery." *The New York Times*, August 8, 2022, https://www.nytimes.com/article/ahmaud-arbery-shooting-georgia.html

103. Diane Duenez, "How Jaywalking has Exposed Racial Bias," *Denver 7 ABC*, September 6, 2022, https://www.denver7.com/news/national/two-americas/how-jaywalking-has-exposed-racial-bias

104. Brave New Films, "Racially Charged: America's Misdemeanor Problem."

105. Brave New Films, "Racially Charged: America's Misdemeanor Problem."

106. Brave New Films, "Racially Charged: America's Misdemeanor Problem."

107. Monica Llorente, "Criminalizing Poverty through Fines, Fees, and Costs," *American Bar Association*. October 3, 2016, https://www.americanbar.org/groups/litigation/committees/childrens-rights/articles/2016/criminalizing-poverty-fines-fees-costs/

108. Brave New Films, "Racially Charged: America's Misdemeanor Problem."

109. Llorente, "Criminalizing Poverty Through Fines, Fees, and Costs."

110. "What Is the Difference Between White Collar Crime and Blue Collar Crime?" *Foley Griffin*, December 16, 2020, https://www.foleygriffin.com/blog/2020/december/what-is-the-difference-between-white-collar-crim/

111. Matt Zbrog, "Follow the Money: Why Financial Crimes often Go Unpunished," *Forensics Colleges*, 2018, https://www.forensicscolleges.com/blog/follow-the-money/unpunished-financial-crimes

112. Alison Diana, "Big Data Plays Arresting Role in White Collar Crime," *EnterpriseAI*, October 1, 2015, https://www.enterpriseai.news/2015/10/01/big-data-plays-arresting-role-in-white-collar-crime/

113. Patricia Jankowski, "Sentencing White Collar Offenders," *Study.com*, January 11, 2018, https://study.com/academy/lesson/sentencing-white-collar-offenders.html

Shanna Van Slyke, and William D. Bales, "A Contemporary Study of the Decision To Incarcerate White-collar and Street Property Offenders," *Punishment & Society*, April 8, 2012, 14(2), 217-246. https://doi.org/10.1177/1462474511434437

114. Zbrog, "Follow the Money: Why Financial Crimes often Go Unpunished."

115. Weir, "Inequality at School: What's Behind the Racial Disparity in Our Education System?"

116a Susan Colantuono, "When You Are Accostomed To Privilege Equality Feels Like Oppression," *Leading Now*, 2023, https://www.leadingnow.biz/blog/when-youre-accustomed-to-privilege-equality-feels-like-oppression

116. Harvard Library, "Scientific Racism," *Harvard Library*, 2023, https://library.harvard.edu/confronting-anti-black-racism/scientific-racism

117. Ben Explain, "What is Redlining? Redlining Explained, A Brief History," *YouTube*, September 18, 2020, https://www.youtube.com/watch?v=w6qvYow9uAY

118. Ben Explain, "What is Redlining? Redlining Explained, A Brief History."

119a "School-To-Prison-Pipeline," *NYCLU*, April, 2023, https://www.nyclu.org/en/issues/racial-justice/school-prison-pipeline

Michael Rocque and Raymond Paternoster, "Understanding the Antecedents of The 'School-To-Jail' link: The Relationship Between Race and School Discipline," *Journal of Criminal Law and Criminology*, vol. 101, no. 2, spring 2011, pp. 633+. *Gale OneFile: LegalTrac*,link.gale.com/apps/doc/A256777964/LT?u=vic_liberty&sid=summon&xid=edc7bb82

119b "Redlining," *Cornell Law School*, April, 2022, https://www.law.cornell.edu/wex/redlining

119. Watson, "How the Media System Fuels Anti-Black Racism."

120. Bell, "What Is Media 2070?"

121. Bell, "What Is Media 2070?"

122. Mallory Moench, "Newspaper Apologizes for 'Shameful' Coverage of Lynchings," *AP News*, April 26, 2018, https://www.washingtonpost.com/national/newspaper-apologizes-for-shameful-coverage-of-lynchings/2018/04/26/cc6bd7a8-499b-11e8-8082-105a446d19b8_story.html

123. "Literacy by any Means Necessary: The History of Anti-Literacy Laws in the U.S.," *Oakland Literacy Coalition*, January 12, 2022, https://oaklandliteracycoalition.org/literacy-by-any-means-necessary-the-history-of-anti-literacy-laws-in-the-u-s/

124. Ariel Jao, "Segregation, School Funding Inequalities still Punishing Black, Latino Students," *NBC News*, January 12, 2018, https://www.nbcnews.com/news/latino/segregation-school-funding-inequalities-still-punishing-black-latino-students-n837186

125. Brave New Films, "Racially Charged: America's Misdemeanor Problem."

126. Tom Jackman, "For a Second Year, Most U.S. Police Departments Decline to Share Information on their Use of Force," *The Washington Post*, June 9, 2021, https://www.washingtonpost.com/nation/2021/06/09/police-use-of-force-data/

127. "Landmark Legislation: The Fourteenth Amendment," *Senate.gov*, https://www.senate.gov/about/origins-foundations/senate-and-constitution/14th-amendment.htm

128. U.S. Department of Housing and Urban Development, "History of Fair Housing," *U.S. Department of Housing and Urban Development*, October 23, 2031, https://www.hud.gov/program_offices/fair_housing_equal_opp/aboutfheo/history

www.ingramcontent.com/pod-product-compliance
Lightning Source LLC
Chambersburg PA
CBHW031219120626
46545CB00003B/905